Document Everything!

The High Conflict Divorced and Single Parent Helper

Fill in Your Own Dates and Track Important Custody and Visitation Details with Child Support and Shared Expense Ledgers Including Event Trackers and Communication Log

Series: Co-Parenting Planners
Book 3
Edition 1

Document Everything! The High Conflict Divorced and Single Parent Helper: Fill in Your Own Dates and Track Important Custody and Visitation Details with Child Support and Shared Expense Ledgers Including Event Trackers and Communication Log

Arisa Williams

keywords: 2019, 2020, 2021, 2022, mid-year, school year, coparenting, co-parenting, duel family, blended family, family relationships, custodial, visiting, agreement, battle, raising children, positive solutions, shared custody, rights, court documentation, documentation, single parenting, support, resource, toolkit, handbook, divorced parents, parents, tasks, sports, travelers, events, teacher, weekly, improve productivity, office, business, agenda, memory, annual tracker, long term goals, previous year review, personal planner, desk size planner, deadlines, deadline, personalized organizer, datebook, scheduling, compact, special events, day to day, writing, small size, pocket size, vertical layout, three year, two year, multiple year, time management, student, blank pages, dot pages, grid dots, track progress, assistant, appointments, dated, journal, notebook, inspiration, diary, day minder, scheduler, activity, activities, long term planners, stationary, Japanese style planner, daily desk diary, day timer, notes, reminder, ideas, plan, life, to do, moon phases, year in review, federal holidays and common observances, any year, undated,

ISBN: 9781077122185

Planner Contents:

- Worksheets to log **Child Support** transactions
  - Log scheduled payments, arrears payments, and interest payments
  - Write down transaction details and totals
  - Keep a record of current child support due

- Children's **Custody/Visitation Calendars**
  - Calendars include Custody vs. Visitation visuals to easily track changes in children's physical placement
  - Notate which parent picks up or drops off
  - Designate time and location of meetings
  - Easily calculate and log hours per month of visitation vs. primary custody
  - Log percentage of visitation and primary physical custody hours
  - Log monthly overnights

- Additional **Personal Monthly Calendars**
  - A second monthly calendar set for your personal monthly schedule
  - Keep children's and parent calendars separate

- Space per individual day for 365 detailed **Daily Entries**

- **Communication Log**
  - Keep a daily record of video chats and phone calls.

- **Shared Expense Tracker**
  - Organize children's shared expenses
  - Record the expense percentage and the dollar amount owed
  - Log the date and notes of reimbursement
  - Track paid payments and reimbursements owed

- List of Yearly **Holiday** Dates
  - 2019, 2020, 2021 and 2022
  - Easy check list for primary custody and visitation for 4 years of holidays and special occasions
  - Includes space to add birthdays and dates for Spring, Summer and Winter Break

- Designate parent claiming children as **dependents by tax year**

- Keep accurate records with **Event Tracker** worksheets
  - Repetitive events easily and quickly recorded for personal and official use
  - Track dates of goals or behaviors on a simple check sheet

- Journal sized paperback planner
  - **Fill in the dates** to suit your personal needs, start any month of any year.
  - 7" x 10" is a **convenient size** for desktop or carrying
  - Personalize the details by adding your own dates and details
  - Keep daily, detailed records of co-parenting and parent/child interaction
  - Perfect for accurately detailed recording of dates, events and transactions
  - Use as a day planner, a journal or a dairy of past events

Holidays
2019 to 2022

Holidays and Observances

2019

C☐ V☐ - **January 1 - New Year's Day**
C☐ V☐ - **January 21 - Martin Luther King, Jr. Day *****
C☐ V☐ - February 2 - Groundhog Day
C☐ V☐ - February 5 - Chinese New Year
C☐ V☐ - February 14 - Valentine's Day
C☐ V☐ - **February 18 - Presidents' Day *****
C☐ V☐ - March 10 - Daylight Savings
C☐ V☐ - March 17 - St. Patrick's Day
C☐ V☐ - March 20 - Spring Equinox
C☐ V☐ - April 1 - April Fool's Day
C☐ V☐ - April 15 - Tax Day
C☐ V☐ - _____ - **Spring Break**
C☐ V☐ - April 19 - Good Friday
C☐ V☐ - April 20 - Passover (First Day0
C☐ V☐ - **April 21 - Easter Sunday**
C☐ V☐ - April 22 - Earth Day
C☐ V☐ - May 5 - Cinco de Mayo
C☐ V☐ - May 6 - Ramadan Starts
C☐ V☐ - **May 12 - Mother's Day**
C☐ V☐ - May 18 - Armed Forces Day
C☐ V☐ - **May 27 - Memorial Day *****
C☐ V☐ - _____ - **Summer Break**
C☐ V☐ - June 14 - Flag Day
C☐ V☐ - **June 16 - Father's Day**
C☐ V☐ - June 19 - Juneteenth
C☐ V☐ - June 21 - Summer Solstice
C☐ V☐ - **July 4 - Independence Day**
C☐ V☐ - **September 2 - Labor Day *****
C☐ V☐ - September 8 - Grandparents' Day
C☐ V☐ - September 11 - Patriot Day
C☐ V☐ - September 23 - Autumnal Equinox
C☐ V☐ - September 27 - Native American Day
C☐ V☐ - October 9 - Yom Kippur
C☐ V☐ - **October 14 - Columbus Day *****
C☐ V☐ - October 19 - Sweetest Day
C☐ V☐ - October 31 - Halloween
C☐ V☐ - November 3 - Daylight Savings
C☐ V☐ - **November 11 - Veterans' Day**
C☐ V☐ - **November 28 - Thanksgiving Day**
C☐ V☐ - December 21 - Winter Solstice
C☐ V☐ - December 23 - Chanukah/Hanukkah (First Day)
C☐ V☐ - _____ - **Winter Break**
C☐ V☐ - **December 24 - Christmas Eve**
C☐ V☐ - **December 25 - Christmas Day**
C☐ V☐ - December 26 - Kwanzaa (First Day)
C☐ V☐ - **December 31 - New Year's Eve**

★ **Special Events**

C☐ - Custodial Parent

V☐ - Visitation

Birthdays and Other Special Occasions
C☐ V☐ - _____
C☐ V☐ - _____
C☐ V☐ - _____
C☐ V☐ - _____
C☐ V☐ - _____

C ☐ V ☐ - **January 1 - New Year's Day**
C ☐ V ☐ - **January 20 - Martin Luther King, Jr. Day**
C ☐ V ☐ - January 25 - Chinese New Year
C ☐ V ☐ - February 2 - Groundhog Day
C ☐ V ☐ - February 14 - Valentine's Day
C ☐ V ☐ - **February 17 - Presidents' Day**
C ☐ V ☐ - March 8 - Daylight Savings
C ☐ V ☐ - March 17 - St. Patrick's Day
C ☐ V ☐ - March 19 - The Spring Equinox
C ☐ V ☐ - April 1 - April Fool's Day
C ☐ V ☐ - April 9 - Passover (First Day)
C ☐ V ☐ - _____ - **Spring Break**
C ☐ V ☐ - April 10 - Good Friday
C ☐ V ☐ - **April 12 - Easter Sunday**
C ☐ V ☐ - April 15 - Tax Day
C ☐ V ☐ - April 24 - Arbor Day
C ☐ V ☐ - April 24 - Ramadan Starts
C ☐ V ☐ - May 5 - Cinco de Mayo
C ☐ V ☐ - **May 10 - Mother's Day**
C ☐ V ☐ - May 16 - Armed Forces Day
C ☐ V ☐ - **May 25 - Memorial Day**
C ☐ V ☐ - _____ - **Summer Break**
C ☐ V ☐ - June 14 - Flag Day
C ☐ V ☐ - June 19 - Juneteenth
C ☐ V ☐ - June 20 - Summer Solstice
C ☐ V ☐ - **June 21 - Father's Day**
C ☐ V ☐ - **July 4 - Independence Day**
C ☐ V ☐ - **September 7 - Labor Day**
C ☐ V ☐ - September 11 - Patriot Day
C ☐ V ☐ - September 13 - Grandparents' Day
C ☐ V ☐ - September 22 - Autumnal Equinox
C ☐ V ☐ - September 25 - Native American Day
C ☐ V ☐ - **October 12 - Columbus Day**
C ☐ V ☐ - October 17 - Sweetest Day
C ☐ V ☐ - October 31 - Halloween
C ☐ V ☐ - November 1 - Daylight Savings
C ☐ V ☐ - November 3 - Election Day
C ☐ V ☐ - **November 11 - Veterans' Day**
C ☐ V ☐ - **November 26 - Thanksgiving Day**
C ☐ V ☐ - December 11 - Chanukah/Hanukkah (First Day)
C ☐ V ☐ - December 21 - Winter Solstice
C ☐ V ☐ - _____ - **Winter Break**
C ☐ V ☐ - **December 24 - Christmas Eve**
C ☐ V ☐ - **December 25 - Christmas Day**
C ☐ V ☐ - December 26 - Kwanzaa (First Day)
C ☐ V ☐ - **December 31 - New Year's Eve**

★ **Special Events**

C ☐ - Custodial Parent

V ☐ - Visitation

Birthdays and Other Special Occasions
C ☐ V ☐ - _____
C ☐ V ☐ - _____
C ☐ V ☐ - _____
C ☐ V ☐ - _____
C ☐ V ☐ - _____

C☐ V☐ - **January 1 - New Year's Day**
C☐ V☐ - **January 18 - Martin Luther King, Jr. Day**
C☐ V☐ - January 20 - Inauguration Day
C☐ V☐ - February 2 - Groundhog Day
C☐ V☐ - February 12 - Chinese New Year
C☐ V☐ - February 14 - Valentine's Day
C☐ V☐ - **February 15 - Presidents' Day**
C☐ V☐ - March 14 - Daylight Savings
C☐ V☐ - March 17 - St. Patrick's Day
C☐ V☐ - March 20 - Spring Equinox
C☐ V☐ - March 28 - Passover (First Day)
C☐ V☐ - April 1 - April Fool's Day
C☐ V☐ - _____ - **Spring Break**
C☐ V☐ - April 2 - Good Friday
C☐ V☐ - **April 4 - Easter Sunday**
C☐ V☐ - April 13 - Ramadan Starts
C☐ V☐ - April 15 - Tax Day
C☐ V☐ - April 30 - Arbor Day
C☐ V☐ - May 5 - Cinco de Mayo
C☐ V☐ - **May 9 - Mother's Day**
C☐ V☐ - May 15 - Armed Forces Day
C☐ V☐ - **May 31 - Memorial Day**
C☐ V☐ - _____ - **Summer Break**
C☐ V☐ - June 14 - Flag Day
C☐ V☐ - June 19 - Juneteenth
C☐ V☐ - June 20 - Summer Solstice
C☐ V☐ - **June 20 - Father's Day**
C☐ V☐ - **July 4 - Independence Day**
C☐ V☐ - **September 6 - Labor Day**
C☐ V☐ - September 11 - Patriot Day
C☐ V☐ - September 12 - Grandparents' Day
C☐ V☐ - September 16 - Yom Kippur
C☐ V☐ - September 22 - Autumnal Equinox
C☐ V☐ - September 24 - Native American Day
C☐ V☐ - **October 11 - Columbus Day**
C☐ V☐ - October 16 - Sweetest Day
C☐ V☐ - October 31 - Halloween
C☐ V☐ - November 7 - Daylight Savings
C☐ V☐ - **November 11 - Veterans' Day**
C☐ V☐ - **November 25 - Thanksgiving Day**
C☐ V☐ - November 29 - Chanukah/Hanukkah (First Day)
C☐ V☐ - December 21 - Winter Solstice
C☐ V☐ - _____ - **Winter Break**
C☐ V☐ - **December 24 - Christmas Eve**
C☐ V☐ - **December 25 - Christmas Day**
C☐ V☐ - December 26 - Kwanzaa (First Day)
C☐ V☐ - **December 31 - New Year's Eve**

★ **Special Events**

C☐ - Custodial Parent

V☐ - Visitation

Birthdays and Other Special Occasions
C☐ V☐ - _____
C☐ V☐ - _____
C☐ V☐ - _____
C☐ V☐ - _____
C☐ V☐ - _____

C☐ V☐ – **January 1 – New Year's Day**
C☐ V☐ – **January 17 – Martin Luther King, Jr. Day**
C☐ V☐ – February 1 – Chinese New Year
C☐ V☐ – February 2 – Groundhog Day
C☐ V☐ – February 14 – Valentine's Day
C☐ V☐ – **February 21 – Presidents' Day**
C☐ V☐ – March 13 – Daylight Savings
C☐ V☐ – March 17 – St. Patrick's Day
C☐ V☐ – March 20 – Spring Equinox
C☐ V☐ – April 1 – April Fool's Day
C☐ V☐ – _____ – **Spring Break**
C☐ V☐ – April 3 – Ramadan Starts
C☐ V☐ – April 15 – Good Friday
C☐ V☐ – April 16 – Passover (First Day)
C☐ V☐ – **April 17 – Easter Sunday**
C☐ V☐ – April 18 – Tax Day
C☐ V☐ – April 29 – Arbor Day
C☐ V☐ – May 5 – Cinco de Mayo
C☐ V☐ – **May 8 – Mother's Day**
C☐ V☐ – May 10 – Primary Election Day
C☐ V☐ – May 21 – Armed Forces Day
C☐ V☐ – **May 30 – Memorial Day**
C☐ V☐ – _____ – **Summer Break**
C☐ V☐ – June 14 – Flag Day
C☐ V☐ – **June 19 – Father's Day**
C☐ V☐ – June 19 – Juneteenth
C☐ V☐ – June 21 – Summer Solstice
C☐ V☐ – **July 4 – Independence Day**
C☐ V☐ – **September 5 – Labor Day**
C☐ V☐ – September 11 – Grandparents' Day
C☐ V☐ – September 11 – Patriot Day
C☐ V☐ – September 22 – Autumnal Equinox
C☐ V☐ – September 23 – Native American Day
C☐ V☐ – October 5 – Yom Kippur
C☐ V☐ – **October 10 – Columbus Day**
C☐ V☐ – October 15 – Sweetest Day
C☐ V☐ – October 31 – Halloween
C☐ V☐ – November 6 – Daylight Savings
C☐ V☐ – Nov 8 – Election Day
C☐ V☐ – **November 11 – Veterans' Day**
C☐ V☐ – **November 24 – Thanksgiving Day**
C☐ V☐ – December 19 – Chanukah/Hanukkah (First Day)
C☐ V☐ – December 21 – Winter Solstice
C☐ V☐ – _____ – **Winter Break**
C☐ V☐ – **December 24 – Christmas Ever**
C☐ V☐ – **December 25 – Christmas Day**
C☐ V☐ – December 26 – Kwanzaa (First Day)
C☐ V☐ – **December 31 – New Year's Eve**

Birthdays and Other Special Occasions

C☐ V☐ – _____
C☐ V☐ – _____
C☐ V☐ – _____
C☐ V☐ – _____
C☐ V☐ – _____

★ Special Events

C☐ – Custodial Parent

V☐ – Visitation

Notes

Visitation & Custody

Hours by Month and Week

January has 31 days = 744 hours
February has 28 or 29 days = 672 or 696 hours
March has 31 days = 744 hours
April has 30 days = 720 hours
May has 31 days = 744 hours
June has 30 days = 720 hours
July has 31 days = 744 hours
ust has 31 days = 744 hours
er has 30 days = 720 hours
has 31 days = 744 hours
has 30 days = 720 hours
as 31 days = 744 hours

Example!

Day Week = 24 Hours
2 Day Week = 48 Hours
3 Day Week = 72 Hours
4 Day Week = 96 Hours
5 Day Week = 120 Hours
6 Day Week = 144 Hours
7 Day Week = 168 Hours

Calculate the Visitation Percentage:

__107__ Visitation Hours ÷ __744__ Total Hours in Month = __.148__ X 100 = __14%__ Visitation %

Calculate the Custody Percentage:

__637__ Custody Hours ÷ __744__ Total Hours in Month = __.856__ X 100 = __85%__ Custody %

Example: 144 Visitation Hours ÷ 744 Total Hours in July = .19 x 100 = 19% Visitation Percentage

Number of Overnights:	Secondary Household Total **Visitation**:	Primary Household Total **Custody**:
5	14%	85%

Month/Year: _Example Month_

Custody / Visitation Schedule

SU	M	T	W	TH	F	SA	Hours
1 Pick Up. **X** Drop Off Location: **House** Transport by: **Dad** Time: **3:00 p.m.**	**2** Pick Up Drop Off Location: Transport by: Time:	**3** Pick Up Drop Off Location: Transport by: Time:	**4** Pick Up Drop Off Location: Transport by: Time:	**5** Pick Up Drop Off Location: Transport by: Time:	**6** Pick Up Drop Off Location: Transport by: Time:	**7** Pick Up Drop Off Location: Transport by: Time:	Hours 15 / 153
C _____ **V** ⊙ ____							
8 Pick Up Drop Off Location: Transport by: Time:	**9** Pick Up Drop Off Location: Transport by: Time:	**10** Pick Up Drop Off Location: Transport by: Time:	**11** Pick Up Drop Off Location: Transport by: Time:	**12** Pick Up Drop Off Location: Transport by: Time:	**13** Pick Up. Drop Off. **X** Location: **Park** Transport by: **Mom** Time: **9:00 a.m.**	**14** Pick Up Drop Off Location: Transport by: Time:	Hours 39 / 129
C _____ **V**					____ ⊙ ____		
15 Pick Up. **X** Drop Off Location: **house** Transport by: **Dad** Time: **1 p.m.**	**16** Pick Up Drop Off Location: Transport by: Time:	**17** Pick Up Drop Off Location: Transport by: Time:	**18** Pick Up Drop Off Location: Transport by: Time:	**19** Pick Up Drop Off Location: Transport by: Time:	**20** Pick Up Drop Off Location: Transport by: Time:	**21** Pick Up Drop Off Location: Transport by: Time:	Hours 13 / 155
C _____ **V** ⊙ __							
22 Pick Up Drop Off Location: Transport by: Time:	**23** Pick Up Drop Off Location: Transport by: Time:	**24** Pick Up Drop Off Location: Transport by: Time:	**25** Pick Up. **X** Drop Off Location: **school** Transport by: **Dad** Time: **3 p.m.**	**26** Pick Up Drop Off Location: Transport by: Time:	**27** Pick Up Drop Off. **X** Location: **school** Transport by: **Dad** Time: **7:00 a.m.**	**28** Pick Up Drop Off Location: Transport by: Time:	Hours 40 / 128
C _____ **V**			⊙ ____ ⊙		_____		
29 Pick Up Drop Off Location: Transport by: Time:	**30** Pick Up Drop Off Location: Transport by: Time:	**31** Pick Up Drop Off Location: Transport by: Time:	Pick Up Drop Off Location: Transport by: Time:	Pick Up Drop Off Location:	Pick Up Drop Off Location: Transport by: Time:	Pick Up Drop Off Location: Transport by: Time:	Hours 0 / 72
C _____ **V**							
Pick Up Drop Off Location: Transport by: Time:	Pick Up Drop Off Location: Transport by: Time:	Pick Up Drop Off Location: Transport by: Time:	Pick Up Drop Off Location: Transport by: Time:	Pick Up Drop Off Location: Transport by: Time:			Hours __ / __
C **V**							

Example!

Monthly Total ___744___ **Custody** ___637___ **Visitation** ___107___ **Hours**

Hours by Month and Week

January has 31 days = 744 hours
February has 28 or 29 days = 672 or 696 hours
March has 31 days = 744 hours
April has 30 days = 720 hours
May has 31 days = 744 hours
June has 30 days = 720 hours
July has 31 days = 744 hours
August has 31 days = 744 hours
September has 30 days = 720 hours
October has 31 days = 744 hours
November has 30 days = 720 hours
December has 31 days = 744 hours

1 Day Week = 24 Hours
2 Day Week = 48 Hours
3 Day Week = 72 Hours
4 Day Week = 96 Hours
5 Day Week = 120 Hours
6 Day Week = 144 Hours
7 Day Week = 168 Hours

Calculate the Visitation Percentage:

_____ Visitation Hours ÷ _____ Total Hours in Month = _____ X 100 = _____ Visitation %

Calculate the Custody Percentage:

_____ Custody Hours ÷ _____ Total Hours in Month = _____ X 100 = _____ Custody %

Example: 144 Visitation Hours ÷ 744 Total Hours in July = .19 x 100 = 19% Visitation Percentage

Number of Overnights:	Secondary Household Total **Visitation**:	Primary Household Total **Custody**:

Month/Year: _____

Custody / Visitation Schedule

	SU	M	T	W	TH	F	SA	
	Pick Up. Drop Off Location: Transport by: Time:	Pick Up Drop Off Location: Transport by: Time:	Pick Up Drop Off Location: Transport by: Time:	Pick Up Drop Off Location: Transport by: Time:	Pick Up Drop Off Location: Transport by: Time:	Pick Up Drop Off Location: Transport by: Time:	Pick Up Drop Off Location: Transport by: Time:	Hours
C V								/
	Pick Up Drop Off Location: Transport by: Time:	Pick Up Drop Off Location: Transport by: Time:	Pick Up Drop Off Location: Transport by: Time:	Pick Up Drop Off Location: Transport by: Time:	Pick Up Drop Off Location: Transport by: Time:	Pick Up. Drop Off. Location: Transport by: Time:	Pick Up Drop Off Location: Transport by: Time:	Hours
C V								/
	Pick Up. X Drop Off Location: house Transport by: Dad Time: 1 p.m.	Pick Up Drop Off Location: Transport by: Time:	Pick Up Drop Off Location: Transport by: Time:	Pick Up Drop Off Location: Transport by: Time:	Pick Up Drop Off Location: Transport by: Time:	Pick Up Drop Off Location: Transport by: Time:	Pick Up Drop Off Location: Transport by: Time:	Hours
C V								/
	Pick Up Drop Off Location: Transport by: Time:	Pick Up Drop Off Location: Transport by: Time:	Pick Up Drop Off Location: Transport by: Time:	Pick Up. Drop Off Location: Transport by: Time:	Pick Up Drop Off Location: Transport by: Time:	Pick Up Drop Off. Location: Transport by: Time:	Pick Up Drop Off Location: Transport by: Time:	Hours
C V								/
	Pick Up Drop Off Location: Transport by: Time:	Pick Up Drop Off Location: Transport by: Time:	Pick Up Drop Off Location: Transport by: Time:	Pick Up Drop Off Location: Transport by: Time:	Pick Up Drop Off Location: Transport by: Time:	Pick Up Drop Off Location: Transport by: Time:	Pick Up Drop Off Location: Transport by: Time:	Hours
C V								/
	Pick Up Drop Off Location: Transport by: Time:	Pick Up Drop Off Location: Transport by: Time:	Pick Up Drop Off Location: Transport by: Time:	Pick Up Drop Off Location: Transport by: Time:	Pick Up Drop Off Location: Transport by: Time:	Pick Up Drop Off Location: Transport by: Time:	Pick Up Drop Off Location: Transport by: Time:	Hours
C V								/

Monthly Total _____   **Custody** _____   **Visitation** _____ **Hours**

Hours by Month and Week

January has 31 days = 744 hours
February has 28 or 29 days = 672 or 696 hours
March has 31 days = 744 hours
April has 30 days = 720 hours
May has 31 days = 744 hours
June has 30 days = 720 hours
July has 31 days = 744 hours
August has 31 days = 744 hours
September has 30 days = 720 hours
October has 31 days = 744 hours
November has 30 days = 720 hours
December has 31 days = 744 hours

1 Day Week = 24 Hours
2 Day Week = 48 Hours
3 Day Week = 72 Hours
4 Day Week = 96 Hours
5 Day Week = 120 Hours
6 Day Week = 144 Hours
7 Day Week = 168 Hours

Calculate the Visitation Percentage:

_____ Visitation Hours ÷ _____ Total Hours in Month = _____ X 100 = _____ Visitation %

Calculate the Custody Percentage:

_____ Custody Hours ÷ _____ Total Hours in Month = _____ X 100 = _____ Custody %

Example: 144 Visitation Hours ÷ 744 Total Hours in July = .19 x 100 = 19% Visitation Percentage

Number of Overnights:	Secondary Household Total **Visitation**:	Primary Household Total **Custody**:

Month/Year: _____

Custody / Visitation Schedule

	SU	M	T	W	TH	F	SA	
	Pick Up. Drop Off Location: Transport by: Time:	Pick Up Drop Off Location: Transport by: Time:	Pick Up Drop Off Location: Transport by: Time:	Pick Up Drop Off Location: Transport by: Time:	Pick Up Drop Off Location: Transport by: Time:	Pick Up Drop Off Location: Transport by: Time:	Pick Up Drop Off Location: Transport by: Time:	Hours
C V								/
	Pick Up Drop Off Location: Transport by: Time:	Pick Up Drop Off Location: Transport by: Time:	Pick Up Drop Off Location: Transport by: Time:	Pick Up Drop Off Location: Transport by: Time:	Pick Up Drop Off Location: Transport by: Time:	Pick Up. Drop Off. Location: Transport by: Time:	Pick Up Drop Off Location: Transport by: Time:	Hours
C V								/
	Pick Up. X Drop Off Location: house Transport by: Dad Time: 1 p.m.	Pick Up Drop Off Location: Transport by: Time:	Pick Up Drop Off Location: Transport by: Time:	Pick Up Drop Off Location: Transport by: Time:	Pick Up Drop Off Location: Transport by: Time:	Pick Up Drop Off Location: Transport by: Time:	Pick Up Drop Off Location: Transport by: Time:	Hours
C V								/
	Pick Up Drop Off Location: Transport by: Time:	Pick Up Drop Off Location: Transport by: Time:	Pick Up Drop Off Location: Transport by: Time:	Pick Up. Drop Off Location: Transport by: Time:	Pick Up Drop Off Location: Transport by: Time:	Pick Up Drop Off. Location: Transport by: Time:	Pick Up Drop Off Location: Transport by: Time:	Hours
C V								/
	Pick Up Drop Off Location: Transport by: Time:	Pick Up Drop Off Location: Transport by: Time:	Pick Up Drop Off Location: Transport by: Time:	Pick Up Drop Off Location: Transport by: Time:	Pick Up Drop Off Location: Transport by: Time:	Pick Up Drop Off Location: Transport by: Time:	Pick Up Drop Off Location: Transport by: Time:	Hours
C V								/
	Pick Up Drop Off Location: Transport by: Time:	Pick Up Drop Off Location: Transport by: Time:	Pick Up Drop Off Location: Transport by: Time:	Pick Up Drop Off Location: Transport by: Time:	Pick Up Drop Off Location: Transport by: Time:	Pick Up Drop Off Location: Transport by: Time:	Pick Up Drop Off Location: Transport by: Time:	Hours
C V								/

Monthly Total _____   **Custody** _____   **Visitation** _____   **Hours**

Hours by Month and Week

January has 31 days = 744 hours
February has 28 or 29 days = 672 or 696 hours
March has 31 days = 744 hours
April has 30 days = 720 hours
May has 31 days = 744 hours
June has 30 days = 720 hours
July has 31 days = 744 hours
August has 31 days = 744 hours
September has 30 days = 720 hours
October has 31 days = 744 hours
November has 30 days = 720 hours
December has 31 days = 744 hours

1 Day Week = 24 Hours
2 Day Week = 48 Hours
3 Day Week = 72 Hours
4 Day Week = 96 Hours
5 Day Week = 120 Hours
6 Day Week = 144 Hours
7 Day Week = 168 Hours

Calculate the Visitation Percentage:

_____ Visitation Hours ÷ _____ Total Hours in Month = _____ X 100 = _____ Visitation %

Calculate the Custody Percentage:

_____ Custody Hours ÷ _____ Total Hours in Month = _____ X 100 = _____ Custody %

Example: 144 Visitation Hours ÷ 744 Total Hours in July = .19 x 100 = 19% Visitation Percentage

Number of Overnights:	Secondary Household Total **Visitation**:	Primary Household Total **Custody**:

Month/Year: _____

	SU	M	T	W	TH	F	SA	Hours
C **V**	Pick Up. Drop Off Location: Transport by: Time:	Pick Up Drop Off Location: Transport by: Time:	Pick Up Drop Off Location: Transport by: Time:	Pick Up Drop Off Location: Transport by: Time:	Pick Up Drop Off Location: Transport by: Time:	Pick Up Drop Off Location: Transport by: Time:	Pick Up Drop Off Location: Transport by: Time:	Hours /
C **V**	Pick Up Drop Off Location: Transport by: Time:	Pick Up Drop Off Location: Transport by: Time:	Pick Up Drop Off Location: Transport by: Time:	Pick Up Drop Off Location: Transport by: Time:	Pick Up Drop Off Location: Transport by: Time:	Pick Up. Drop Off. Location: Transport by: Time:	Pick Up Drop Off Location: Transport by: Time:	Hours /
C **V**	Pick Up. X Drop Off Location: house Transport by: Dad Time: 1 p.m.	Pick Up Drop Off Location: Transport by: Time:	Pick Up Drop Off Location: Transport by: Time:	Pick Up Drop Off Location: Transport by: Time:	Pick Up Drop Off Location: Transport by: Time:	Pick Up Drop Off Location: Transport by: Time:	Pick Up Drop Off Location: Transport by: Time:	Hours /
C **V**	Pick Up Drop Off Location: Transport by: Time:	Pick Up Drop Off Location: Transport by: Time:	Pick Up Drop Off Location: Transport by: Time:	Pick Up. Drop Off Location: Transport by: Time:	Pick Up Drop Off Location: Transport by: Time:	Pick Up Drop Off. Location: Transport by: Time:	Pick Up Drop Off Location: Transport by: Time:	Hours /
C **V**	Pick Up Drop Off Location: Transport by: Time:	Pick Up Drop Off Location: Transport by: Time:	Pick Up Drop Off Location: Transport by: Time:	Pick Up Drop Off Location: Transport by: Time:	Pick Up Drop Off Location: Transport by: Time:	Pick Up Drop Off Location: Transport by: Time:	Pick Up Drop Off Location: Transport by: Time:	Hours /
C **V**	Pick Up Drop Off Location: Transport by: Time:	Pick Up Drop Off Location: Transport by: Time:	Pick Up Drop Off Location: Transport by: Time:	Pick Up Drop Off Location: Transport by: Time:	Pick Up Drop Off Location: Transport by: Time:	Pick Up Drop Off Location: Transport by: Time:	Pick Up Drop Off Location: Transport by: Time:	Hours /

Monthly Total _____   **Custody** _____   **Visitation** _____   **Hours**

Hours by Month and Week

January has 31 days = 744 hours
February has 28 or 29 days = 672 or 696 hours
March has 31 days = 744 hours
April has 30 days = 720 hours
May has 31 days = 744 hours
June has 30 days = 720 hours
July has 31 days = 744 hours
August has 31 days = 744 hours
September has 30 days = 720 hours
October has 31 days = 744 hours
November has 30 days = 720 hours
December has 31 days = 744 hours

1 Day Week = 24 Hours
2 Day Week = 48 Hours
3 Day Week = 72 Hours
4 Day Week = 96 Hours
5 Day Week = 120 Hours
6 Day Week = 144 Hours
7 Day Week = 168 Hours

Calculate the Visitation Percentage:

_____ Visitation Hours ÷ _____ Total Hours in Month = _____ X 100 = _____ Visitation %

Calculate the Custody Percentage:

_____ Custody Hours ÷ _____ Total Hours in Month = _____ X 100 = _____ Custody %

Example: 144 Visitation Hours ÷ 744 Total Hours in July = .19 x 100 = 19% Visitation Percentage

Number of Overnights:	Secondary Household Total **Visitation**:	Primary Household Total **Custody**:

Month/Year: _____

Custody / Visitation Schedule

	SU	M	T	W	TH	F	SA	
C **V**	Pick Up. Drop Off Location: Transport by: Time:	Pick Up Drop Off Location: Transport by: Time:	Pick Up Drop Off Location: Transport by: Time:	Pick Up Drop Off Location: Transport by: Time:	Pick Up Drop Off Location: Transport by: Time:	Pick Up Drop Off Location: Transport by: Time:	Pick Up Drop Off Location: Transport by: Time:	Hours
C **V**	Pick Up Drop Off Location: Transport by: Time:	Pick Up Drop Off Location: Transport by: Time:	Pick Up Drop Off Location: Transport by: Time:	Pick Up Drop Off Location: Transport by: Time:	Pick Up Drop Off Location: Transport by: Time:	Pick Up. Drop Off. Location: Transport by: Time:	Pick Up Drop Off Location: Transport by: Time:	Hours
C **V**	Pick Up. X Drop Off Location: house Transport by: Dad Time: 1 p.m.	Pick Up Drop Off Location: Transport by: Time:	Pick Up Drop Off Location: Transport by: Time:	Pick Up Drop Off Location: Transport by: Time:	Pick Up Drop Off Location: Transport by: Time:	Pick Up Drop Off Location: Transport by: Time:	Pick Up Drop Off Location: Transport by: Time:	Hours
C **V**	Pick Up Drop Off Location: Transport by: Time:	Pick Up Drop Off Location: Transport by: Time:	Pick Up Drop Off Location: Transport by: Time:	Pick Up. Drop Off Location: Transport by: Time:	Pick Up Drop Off Location: Transport by: Time:	Pick Up Drop Off. Location: Transport by: Time:	Pick Up Drop Off Location: Transport by: Time:	Hours
C **V**	Pick Up Drop Off Location: Transport by: Time:	Pick Up Drop Off Location: Transport by: Time:	Pick Up Drop Off Location: Transport by: Time:	Pick Up Drop Off Location: Transport by: Time:	Pick Up Drop Off Location: Transport by: Time:	Pick Up Drop Off Location: Transport by: Time:	Pick Up Drop Off Location: Transport by: Time:	Hours
C **V**	Pick Up Drop Off Location: Transport by: Time:	Pick Up Drop Off Location: Transport by: Time:	Pick Up Drop Off Location: Transport by: Time:	Pick Up Drop Off Location: Transport by: Time:	Pick Up Drop Off Location: Transport by: Time:	Pick Up Drop Off Location: Transport by: Time:	Pick Up Drop Off Location: Transport by: Time:	Hours

Monthly Total _____   **Custody** _____   **Visitation** _____   **Hours**

Hours by Month and Week

January has 31 days = 744 hours
February has 28 or 29 days = 672 or 696 hours
March has 31 days = 744 hours
April has 30 days = 720 hours
May has 31 days = 744 hours
June has 30 days = 720 hours
July has 31 days = 744 hours
August has 31 days = 744 hours
September has 30 days = 720 hours
October has 31 days = 744 hours
November has 30 days = 720 hours
December has 31 days = 744 hours

1 Day Week = 24 Hours
2 Day Week = 48 Hours
3 Day Week = 72 Hours
4 Day Week = 96 Hours
5 Day Week = 120 Hours
6 Day Week = 144 Hours
7 Day Week = 168 Hours

Calculate the Visitation Percentage:

_____ Visitation Hours ÷ _____ Total Hours in Month = _____ X 100 = _____ Visitation %

Calculate the Custody Percentage:

_____ Custody Hours ÷ _____ Total Hours in Month = _____ X 100 = _____ Custody %

Example: 144 Visitation Hours ÷ 744 Total Hours in July = .19 x 100 = 19% Visitation Percentage

Number of Overnights:	Secondary Household Total **Visitation**:	Primary Household Total **Custody**:

Month/Year:_____

Custody / Visitation Schedule

	SU	M	T	W	TH	F	SA	
C **V**	Pick Up. Drop Off Location: Transport by: Time:	Pick Up Drop Off Location: Transport by: Time:	Pick Up Drop Off Location: Transport by: Time:	Pick Up Drop Off Location: Transport by: Time:	Pick Up Drop Off Location: Transport by: Time:	Pick Up Drop Off Location: Transport by: Time:	Pick Up Drop Off Location: Transport by: Time:	Hours / __
C **V**	Pick Up Drop Off Location: Transport by: Time:	Pick Up Drop Off Location: Transport by: Time:	Pick Up Drop Off Location: Transport by: Time:	Pick Up Drop Off Location: Transport by: Time:	Pick Up Drop Off Location: Transport by: Time:	Pick Up. Drop Off. Location: Transport by: Time:	Pick Up Drop Off Location: Transport by: Time:	Hours / __
C **V**	Pick Up. X Drop Off Location: house Transport by: Dad Time: 1 p.m.	Pick Up Drop Off Location: Transport by: Time:	Pick Up Drop Off Location: Transport by: Time:	Pick Up Drop Off Location: Transport by: Time:	Pick Up Drop Off Location: Transport by: Time:	Pick Up Drop Off Location: Transport by: Time:	Pick Up Drop Off Location: Transport by: Time:	Hours / __
C **V**	Pick Up Drop Off Location: Transport by: Time:	Pick Up Drop Off Location: Transport by: Time:	Pick Up Drop Off Location: Transport by: Time:	Pick Up. Drop Off Location: Transport by: Time:	Pick Up Drop Off Location: Transport by: Time:	Pick Up Drop Off. Location: Transport by: Time:	Pick Up Drop Off Location: Transport by: Time:	Hours / __
C **V**	Pick Up Drop Off Location: Transport by: Time:	Pick Up Drop Off Location: Transport by: Time:	Pick Up Drop Off Location: Transport by: Time:	Pick Up Drop Off Location: Transport by: Time:	Pick Up Drop Off Location: Transport by: Time:	Pick Up Drop Off Location: Transport by: Time:	Pick Up Drop Off Location: Transport by: Time:	Hours / __
C **V**	Pick Up Drop Off Location: Transport by: Time:	Pick Up Drop Off Location: Transport by: Time:	Pick Up Drop Off Location: Transport by: Time:	Pick Up Drop Off Location: Transport by: Time:	Pick Up Drop Off Location: Transport by: Time:	Pick Up Drop Off Location: Transport by: Time:	Pick Up Drop Off Location: Transport by: Time:	Hours / __

Monthly Total _____   **Custody** _____   **Visitation** _____ **Hours**

Hours by Month and Week

January has 31 days = 744 hours
February has 28 or 29 days = 672 or 696 hours
March has 31 days = 744 hours
April has 30 days = 720 hours
May has 31 days = 744 hours
June has 30 days = 720 hours
July has 31 days = 744 hours
August has 31 days = 744 hours
September has 30 days = 720 hours
October has 31 days = 744 hours
November has 30 days = 720 hours
December has 31 days = 744 hours

1 Day Week = 24 Hours
2 Day Week = 48 Hours
3 Day Week = 72 Hours
4 Day Week = 96 Hours
5 Day Week = 120 Hours
6 Day Week = 144 Hours
7 Day Week = 168 Hours

Calculate the Visitation Percentage:

_____ Visitation Hours ÷ _____ Total Hours in Month = _____ X 100 = _____ Visitation %

Calculate the Custody Percentage:

_____ Custody Hours ÷ _____ Total Hours in Month = _____ X 100 = _____ Custody %

Example: 144 Visitation Hours ÷ 744 Total Hours in July = .19 x 100 = 19% Visitation Percentage

Number of Overnights:	Secondary Household Total **Visitation**:	Primary Household Total **Custody**:

Month/Year: _____

Custody / Visitation Schedule

	SU	M	T	W	TH	F	SA	
	Pick Up. Drop Off Location: Transport by: Time:	Pick Up Drop Off Location: Transport by: Time:	Pick Up Drop Off Location: Transport by: Time:	Pick Up Drop Off Location: Transport by: Time:	Pick Up Drop Off Location: Transport by: Time:	Pick Up Drop Off Location: Transport by: Time:	Pick Up Drop Off Location: Transport by: Time:	Hours
C **V**								
	Pick Up Drop Off Location: Transport by: Time:	Pick Up Drop Off Location: Transport by: Time:	Pick Up Drop Off Location: Transport by: Time:	Pick Up Drop Off Location: Transport by: Time:	Pick Up Drop Off Location: Transport by: Time:	Pick Up. Drop Off. Location: Transport by: Time:	Pick Up Drop Off Location: Transport by: Time:	Hours
C **V**								
	Pick Up. X Drop Off Location: house Transport by: Dad Time: 1 p.m.	Pick Up Drop Off Location: Transport by: Time:	Pick Up Drop Off Location: Transport by: Time:	Pick Up Drop Off Location: Transport by: Time:	Pick Up Drop Off Location: Transport by: Time:	Pick Up Drop Off Location: Transport by: Time:	Pick Up Drop Off Location: Transport by: Time:	Hours
C **V**								
	Pick Up Drop Off Location: Transport by: Time:	Pick Up Drop Off Location: Transport by: Time:	Pick Up Drop Off Location: Transport by: Time:	Pick Up. Drop Off Location: Transport by: Time:	Pick Up Drop Off Location: Transport by: Time:	Pick Up Drop Off. Location: Transport by: Time:	Pick Up Drop Off Location: Transport by: Time:	Hours
C **V**								
	Pick Up Drop Off Location: Transport by: Time:	Pick Up Drop Off Location: Transport by: Time:	Pick Up Drop Off Location: Transport by: Time:	Pick Up Drop Off Location: Transport by: Time:	Pick Up Drop Off Location: Transport by: Time:	Pick Up Drop Off Location: Transport by: Time:	Pick Up Drop Off Location: Transport by: Time:	Hours
C **V**								
	Pick Up Drop Off Location: Transport by: Time:	Pick Up Drop Off Location: Transport by: Time:	Pick Up Drop Off Location: Transport by: Time:	Pick Up Drop Off Location: Transport by: Time:	Pick Up Drop Off Location: Transport by: Time:	Pick Up Drop Off Location: Transport by: Time:	Pick Up Drop Off Location: Transport by: Time:	Hours
C **V**								

Monthly Total _____   **Custody** _____   **Visitation** _____ **Hours**

Hours by Month and Week

January has 31 days = 744 hours
February has 28 or 29 days = 672 or 696 hours
March has 31 days = 744 hours
April has 30 days = 720 hours
May has 31 days = 744 hours
June has 30 days = 720 hours
July has 31 days = 744 hours
August has 31 days = 744 hours
September has 30 days = 720 hours
October has 31 days = 744 hours
November has 30 days = 720 hours
December has 31 days = 744 hours

1 Day Week = 24 Hours
2 Day Week = 48 Hours
3 Day Week = 72 Hours
4 Day Week = 96 Hours
5 Day Week = 120 Hours
6 Day Week = 144 Hours
7 Day Week = 168 Hours

Calculate the Visitation Percentage:

_____ Visitation Hours ÷ _____ Total Hours in Month = _____ X 100 = _____ Visitation %

Calculate the Custody Percentage:

_____ Custody Hours ÷ _____ Total Hours in Month = _____ X 100 = _____ Custody %

Example: 144 Visitation Hours ÷ 744 Total Hours in July = .19 x 100 = 19% Visitation Percentage

Number of Overnights:	Secondary Household Total **Visitation**:	Primary Household Total **Custody**:

Month/Year: _____

	SU	M	T	W	TH	F	SA	
	Pick Up. Drop Off Location: Transport by: Time:	Pick Up Drop Off Location: Transport by: Time:	Pick Up Drop Off Location: Transport by: Time:	Pick Up Drop Off Location: Transport by: Time:	Pick Up Drop Off Location: Transport by: Time:	Pick Up Drop Off Location: Transport by: Time:	Pick Up Drop Off Location: Transport by: Time:	Hours
C V								
	Pick Up Drop Off Location: Transport by: Time:	Pick Up Drop Off Location: Transport by: Time:	Pick Up Drop Off Location: Transport by: Time:	Pick Up Drop Off Location: Transport by: Time:	Pick Up Drop Off Location: Transport by: Time:	Pick Up. Drop Off. Location: Transport by: Time:	Pick Up Drop Off Location: Transport by: Time:	Hours
C V								
	Pick Up. X Drop Off Location: house Transport by: Dad Time: 1 p.m.	Pick Up Drop Off Location: Transport by: Time:	Pick Up Drop Off Location: Transport by: Time:	Pick Up Drop Off Location: Transport by: Time:	Pick Up Drop Off Location: Transport by: Time:	Pick Up Drop Off Location: Transport by: Time:	Pick Up Drop Off Location: Transport by: Time:	Hours
C V								
	Pick Up Drop Off Location: Transport by: Time:	Pick Up Drop Off Location: Transport by: Time:	Pick Up Drop Off Location: Transport by: Time:	Pick Up. Drop Off Location: Transport by: Time:	Pick Up Drop Off Location: Transport by: Time:	Pick Up Drop Off. Location: Transport by: Time:	Pick Up Drop Off Location: Transport by: Time:	Hours
C V								
	Pick Up Drop Off Location: Transport by: Time:	Pick Up Drop Off Location: Transport by: Time:	Pick Up Drop Off Location: Transport by: Time:	Pick Up Drop Off Location: Transport by: Time:	Pick Up Drop Off Location: Transport by: Time:	Pick Up Drop Off Location: Transport by: Time:	Pick Up Drop Off Location: Transport by: Time:	Hours
C V								
	Pick Up Drop Off Location: Transport by: Time:	Pick Up Drop Off Location: Transport by: Time:	Pick Up Drop Off Location: Transport by: Time:	Pick Up Drop Off Location: Transport by: Time:	Pick Up Drop Off Location: Transport by: Time:	Pick Up Drop Off Location: Transport by: Time:	Pick Up Drop Off Location: Transport by: Time:	Hours
C V								

Monthly Total _____ **Custody** _____ **Visitation** _____ **Hours**

Hours by Month and Week

January has 31 days = 744 hours
February has 28 or 29 days = 672 or 696 hours
March has 31 days = 744 hours
April has 30 days = 720 hours
May has 31 days = 744 hours
June has 30 days = 720 hours
July has 31 days = 744 hours
August has 31 days = 744 hours
September has 30 days = 720 hours
October has 31 days = 744 hours
November has 30 days = 720 hours
December has 31 days = 744 hours

1 Day Week = 24 Hours
2 Day Week = 48 Hours
3 Day Week = 72 Hours
4 Day Week = 96 Hours
5 Day Week = 120 Hours
6 Day Week = 144 Hours
7 Day Week = 168 Hours

Calculate the Visitation Percentage:

_____ Visitation Hours ÷ _____ Total Hours in Month = _____ X 100 = _____ Visitation %

Calculate the Custody Percentage:

_____ Custody Hours ÷ _____ Total Hours in Month = _____ X 100 = _____ Custody %

Example: 144 Visitation Hours ÷ 744 Total Hours in July = .19 x 100 = 19% Visitation Percentage

Number of Overnights:	Secondary Household Total **Visitation**:	Primary Household Total **Custody**:

Month/Year: _____

	SU	M	T	W	TH	F	SA	
	Pick Up. Drop Off Location: Transport by: Time:	Pick Up Drop Off Location: Transport by: Time:	Pick Up Drop Off Location: Transport by: Time:	Pick Up Drop Off Location: Transport by: Time:	Pick Up Drop Off Location: Transport by: Time:	Pick Up Drop Off Location: Transport by: Time:	Pick Up Drop Off Location: Transport by: Time:	Hours ___ ___
C V								
	Pick Up Drop Off Location: Transport by: Time:	Pick Up Drop Off Location: Transport by: Time:	Pick Up Drop Off Location: Transport by: Time:	Pick Up Drop Off Location: Transport by: Time:	Pick Up Drop Off Location: Transport by: Time:	Pick Up. Drop Off. Location: Transport by: Time:	Pick Up Drop Off Location: Transport by: Time:	Hours ___ ___
C V								
	Pick Up. X Drop Off Location: house Transport by: Dad Time: 1 p.m.	Pick Up Drop Off Location: Transport by: Time:	Pick Up Drop Off Location: Transport by: Time:	Pick Up Drop Off Location: Transport by: Time:	Pick Up Drop Off Location: Transport by: Time:	Pick Up Drop Off Location: Transport by: Time:	Pick Up Drop Off Location: Transport by: Time:	Hours ___ ___
C V								
	Pick Up Drop Off Location: Transport by: Time:	Pick Up Drop Off Location: Transport by: Time:	Pick Up Drop Off Location: Transport by: Time:	Pick Up. Drop Off Location: Transport by: Time:	Pick Up Drop Off Location: Transport by: Time:	Pick Up Drop Off. Location: Transport by: Time:	Pick Up Drop Off Location: Transport by: Time:	Hours ___ ___
C V								
	Pick Up Drop Off Location: Transport by: Time:	Pick Up Drop Off Location: Transport by: Time:	Pick Up Drop Off Location: Transport by: Time:	Pick Up Drop Off Location: Transport by: Time:	Pick Up Drop Off Location: Transport by: Time:	Pick Up Drop Off Location: Transport by: Time:	Pick Up Drop Off Location: Transport by: Time:	Hours ___ ___
C V								
	Pick Up Drop Off Location: Transport by: Time:	Pick Up Drop Off Location: Transport by: Time:	Pick Up Drop Off Location: Transport by: Time:	Pick Up Drop Off Location: Transport by: Time:	Pick Up Drop Off Location: Transport by: Time:	Pick Up Drop Off Location: Transport by: Time:	Pick Up Drop Off Location: Transport by: Time:	Hours ___ ___
C V								

Monthly Total _____ **Custody** _____ **Visitation** _____ **Hours**

Hours by Month and Week

January has 31 days = 744 hours
February has 28 or 29 days = 672 or 696 hours
March has 31 days = 744 hours
April has 30 days = 720 hours
May has 31 days = 744 hours
June has 30 days = 720 hours
July has 31 days = 744 hours
August has 31 days = 744 hours
September has 30 days = 720 hours
October has 31 days = 744 hours
November has 30 days = 720 hours
December has 31 days = 744 hours

1 Day Week = 24 Hours
2 Day Week = 48 Hours
3 Day Week = 72 Hours
4 Day Week = 96 Hours
5 Day Week = 120 Hours
6 Day Week = 144 Hours
7 Day Week = 168 Hours

Calculate the Visitation Percentage:

_____ Visitation Hours ÷ _____ Total Hours in Month = _____ X 100 = _____ Visitation %

Calculate the Custody Percentage:

_____ Custody Hours ÷ _____ Total Hours in Month = _____ X 100 = _____ Custody %

Example: 144 Visitation Hours ÷ 744 Total Hours in July = .19 x 100 = 19% Visitation Percentage

Number of Overnights:	Secondary Household Total **Visitation**:	Primary Household Total **Custody**:

Month/Year: _____

Custody / Visitation Schedule

	SU	M	T	W	TH	F	SA	
C V	Pick Up. Drop Off Location: Transport by: Time:	Pick Up Drop Off Location: Transport by: Time:	Pick Up Drop Off Location: Transport by: Time:	Pick Up Drop Off Location: Transport by: Time:	Pick Up Drop Off Location: Transport by: Time:	Pick Up Drop Off Location: Transport by: Time:	Pick Up Drop Off Location: Transport by: Time:	Hours ___ / ___
C V	Pick Up Drop Off Location: Transport by: Time:	Pick Up Drop Off Location: Transport by: Time:	Pick Up Drop Off Location: Transport by: Time:	Pick Up Drop Off Location: Transport by: Time:	Pick Up Drop Off Location: Transport by: Time:	Pick Up. Drop Off. Location: Transport by: Time:	Pick Up Drop Off Location: Transport by: Time:	Hours ___ / ___
C V	Pick Up. X Drop Off Location: house Transport by: Dad Time: 1 p.m.	Pick Up Drop Off Location: Transport by: Time:	Pick Up Drop Off Location: Transport by: Time:	Pick Up Drop Off Location: Transport by: Time:	Pick Up Drop Off Location: Transport by: Time:	Pick Up Drop Off Location: Transport by: Time:	Pick Up Drop Off Location: Transport by: Time:	Hours ___ / ___
C V	Pick Up Drop Off Location: Transport by: Time:	Pick Up Drop Off Location: Transport by: Time:	Pick Up Drop Off Location: Transport by: Time:	Pick Up. Drop Off Location: Transport by: Time:	Pick Up Drop Off Location: Transport by: Time:	Pick Up Drop Off. Location: Transport by: Time:	Pick Up Drop Off Location: Transport by: Time:	Hours ___ / ___
C V	Pick Up Drop Off Location: Transport by: Time:	Pick Up Drop Off Location: Transport by: Time:	Pick Up Drop Off Location: Transport by: Time:	Pick Up Drop Off Location: Transport by: Time:	Pick Up Drop Off Location: Transport by: Time:	Pick Up Drop Off Location: Transport by: Time:	Pick Up Drop Off Location: Transport by: Time:	Hours ___ / ___
C V	Pick Up Drop Off Location: Transport by: Time:	Pick Up Drop Off Location: Transport by: Time:	Pick Up Drop Off Location: Transport by: Time:	Pick Up Drop Off Location: Transport by: Time:	Pick Up Drop Off Location: Transport by: Time:	Pick Up Drop Off Location: Transport by: Time:	Pick Up Drop Off Location: Transport by: Time:	Hours ___ / ___

Monthly Total _____   **Custody** _____   **Visitation** _____ **Hours**

Hours by Month and Week

January has 31 days = 744 hours
February has 28 or 29 days = 672 or 696 hours
March has 31 days = 744 hours
April has 30 days = 720 hours
May has 31 days = 744 hours
June has 30 days = 720 hours
July has 31 days = 744 hours
August has 31 days = 744 hours
September has 30 days = 720 hours
October has 31 days = 744 hours
November has 30 days = 720 hours
December has 31 days = 744 hours

1 Day Week = 24 Hours
2 Day Week = 48 Hours
3 Day Week = 72 Hours
4 Day Week = 96 Hours
5 Day Week = 120 Hours
6 Day Week = 144 Hours
7 Day Week = 168 Hours

Calculate the Visitation Percentage:

_____ Visitation Hours ÷ _____ Total Hours in Month = _____ X 100 = _____ Visitation %

Calculate the Custody Percentage:

_____ Custody Hours ÷ _____ Total Hours in Month = _____ X 100 = _____ Custody %

Example: 144 Visitation Hours ÷ 744 Total Hours in July = .19 x 100 = 19% Visitation Percentage

Number of Overnights:	Secondary Household Total **Visitation**:	Primary Household Total **Custody**:

Month/Year: _____

	SU	M	T	W	TH	F	SA	
	Pick Up. Drop Off Location: Transport by: Time:	Pick Up Drop Off Location: Transport by: Time:	Pick Up Drop Off Location: Transport by: Time:	Pick Up Drop Off Location: Transport by: Time:	Pick Up Drop Off Location: Transport by: Time:	Pick Up Drop Off Location: Transport by: Time:	Pick Up Drop Off Location: Transport by: Time:	Hours
C **V**								/
	Pick Up Drop Off Location: Transport by: Time:	Pick Up Drop Off Location: Transport by: Time:	Pick Up Drop Off Location: Transport by: Time:	Pick Up Drop Off Location: Transport by: Time:	Pick Up Drop Off Location: Transport by: Time:	Pick Up. Drop Off. Location: Transport by: Time:	Pick Up Drop Off Location: Transport by: Time:	Hours
C **V**								/
	Pick Up. X Drop Off Location: house Transport by: Dad Time: 1 p.m.	Pick Up Drop Off Location: Transport by: Time:	Pick Up Drop Off Location: Transport by: Time:	Pick Up Drop Off Location: Transport by: Time:	Pick Up Drop Off Location: Transport by: Time:	Pick Up Drop Off Location: Transport by: Time:	Pick Up Drop Off Location: Transport by: Time:	Hours
C **V**								/
	Pick Up Drop Off Location: Transport by: Time:	Pick Up Drop Off Location: Transport by: Time:	Pick Up Drop Off Location: Transport by: Time:	Pick Up. Drop Off Location: Transport by: Time:	Pick Up Drop Off Location: Transport by: Time:	Pick Up Drop Off. Location: Transport by: Time:	Pick Up Drop Off Location: Transport by: Time:	Hours
C **V**								/
	Pick Up Drop Off Location: Transport by: Time:	Pick Up Drop Off Location: Transport by: Time:	Pick Up Drop Off Location: Transport by: Time:	Pick Up Drop Off Location: Transport by: Time:	Pick Up Drop Off Location: Transport by: Time:	Pick Up Drop Off Location: Transport by: Time:	Pick Up Drop Off Location: Transport by: Time:	Hours
C **V**								/
	Pick Up Drop Off Location: Transport by: Time:	Pick Up Drop Off Location: Transport by: Time:	Pick Up Drop Off Location: Transport by: Time:	Pick Up Drop Off Location: Transport by: Time:	Pick Up Drop Off Location: Transport by: Time:	Pick Up Drop Off Location: Transport by: Time:	Pick Up Drop Off Location: Transport by: Time:	Hours
C **V**								/

Monthly Total _____ **Custody** _____ **Visitation** _____ **Hours**

Hours by Month and Week

January has 31 days = 744 hours
February has 28 or 29 days = 672 or 696 hours
March has 31 days = 744 hours
April has 30 days = 720 hours
May has 31 days = 744 hours
June has 30 days = 720 hours
July has 31 days = 744 hours
August has 31 days = 744 hours
September has 30 days = 720 hours
October has 31 days = 744 hours
November has 30 days = 720 hours
December has 31 days = 744 hours

1 Day Week = 24 Hours
2 Day Week = 48 Hours
3 Day Week = 72 Hours
4 Day Week = 96 Hours
5 Day Week = 120 Hours
6 Day Week = 144 Hours
7 Day Week = 168 Hours

Calculate the Visitation Percentage:

_____ Visitation Hours ÷ _____ Total Hours in Month = _____ X 100 = _____ Visitation %

Calculate the Custody Percentage:

_____ Custody Hours ÷ _____ Total Hours in Month = _____ X 100 = _____ Custody %

Example: 144 Visitation Hours ÷ 744 Total Hours in July = .19 x 100 = 19% Visitation Percentage

Number of Overnights:	Secondary Household Total **Visitation**:	Primary Household Total **Custody**:

Month/Year:_____

Custody / Visitation Schedule

	SU	M	T	W	TH	F	SA	Hours
C **V**	Pick Up. Drop Off Location: Transport by: Time:	Pick Up Drop Off Location: Transport by: Time:	Pick Up Drop Off Location: Transport by: Time:	Pick Up Drop Off Location: Transport by: Time:	Pick Up Drop Off Location: Transport by: Time:	Pick Up Drop Off Location: Transport by: Time:	Pick Up Drop Off Location: Transport by: Time:	Hours ___ / ___
C **V**	Pick Up Drop Off Location: Transport by: Time:	Pick Up Drop Off Location: Transport by: Time:	Pick Up Drop Off Location: Transport by: Time:	Pick Up Drop Off Location: Transport by: Time:	Pick Up Drop Off Location: Transport by: Time:	Pick Up. Drop Off. Location: Transport by: Time:	Pick Up Drop Off Location: Transport by: Time:	Hours ___ / ___
C **V**	Pick Up. X Drop Off Location: house Transport by: Dad Time: 1 p.m.	Pick Up Drop Off Location: Transport by: Time:	Pick Up Drop Off Location: Transport by: Time:	Pick Up Drop Off Location: Transport by: Time:	Pick Up Drop Off Location: Transport by: Time:	Pick Up Drop Off Location: Transport by: Time:	Pick Up Drop Off Location: Transport by: Time:	Hours ___ / ___
C **V**	Pick Up Drop Off Location: Transport by: Time:	Pick Up Drop Off Location: Transport by: Time:	Pick Up Drop Off Location: Transport by: Time:	Pick Up. Drop Off Location: Transport by: Time:	Pick Up Drop Off Location: Transport by: Time:	Pick Up Drop Off. Location: Transport by: Time:	Pick Up Drop Off Location: Transport by: Time:	Hours ___ / ___
C **V**	Pick Up Drop Off Location: Transport by: Time:	Pick Up Drop Off Location: Transport by: Time:	Pick Up Drop Off Location: Transport by: Time:	Pick Up Drop Off Location: Transport by: Time:	Pick Up Drop Off Location: Transport by: Time:	Pick Up Drop Off Location: Transport by: Time:	Pick Up Drop Off Location: Transport by: Time:	Hours ___ / ___
C **V**	Pick Up Drop Off Location: Transport by: Time:	Pick Up Drop Off Location: Transport by: Time:	Pick Up Drop Off Location: Transport by: Time:	Pick Up Drop Off Location: Transport by: Time:	Pick Up Drop Off Location: Transport by: Time:	Pick Up Drop Off Location: Transport by: Time:	Pick Up Drop Off Location: Transport by: Time:	Hours ___ / ___

Monthly Total _____   **Custody** _____   **Visitation** _____   **Hours**

Hours by Month and Week

January has 31 days = 744 hours
February has 28 or 29 days = 672 or 696 hours
March has 31 days = 744 hours
April has 30 days = 720 hours
May has 31 days = 744 hours
June has 30 days = 720 hours
July has 31 days = 744 hours
August has 31 days = 744 hours
September has 30 days = 720 hours
October has 31 days = 744 hours
November has 30 days = 720 hours
December has 31 days = 744 hours

1 Day Week = 24 Hours
2 Day Week = 48 Hours
3 Day Week = 72 Hours
4 Day Week = 96 Hours
5 Day Week = 120 Hours
6 Day Week = 144 Hours
7 Day Week = 168 Hours

Calculate the Visitation Percentage:

_____ Visitation Hours ÷ _____ Total Hours in Month = _____ X 100 = _____ Visitation %

Calculate the Custody Percentage:

_____ Custody Hours ÷ _____ Total Hours in Month = _____ X 100 = _____ Custody %

Example: 144 Visitation Hours ÷ 744 Total Hours in July = .19 x 100 = 19% Visitation Percentage

Number of Overnights:	Secondary Household Total **Visitation**:	Primary Household Total **Custody**:

Month/Year: _____

	SU	M	T	W	TH	F	SA	
	Pick Up. Drop Off Location: Transport by: Time:	Pick Up Drop Off Location: Transport by: Time:	Pick Up Drop Off Location: Transport by: Time:	Pick Up Drop Off Location: Transport by: Time:	Pick Up Drop Off Location: Transport by: Time:	Pick Up Drop Off Location: Transport by: Time:	Pick Up Drop Off Location: Transport by: Time:	Hours ___
C V								
	Pick Up Drop Off Location: Transport by: Time:	Pick Up Drop Off Location: Transport by: Time:	Pick Up Drop Off Location: Transport by: Time:	Pick Up Drop Off Location: Transport by: Time:	Pick Up Drop Off Location: Transport by: Time:	Pick Up. Drop Off. Location: Transport by: Time:	Pick Up Drop Off Location: Transport by: Time:	Hours ___
C V								
	Pick Up. X Drop Off Location: house Transport by: Dad Time: 1 p.m.	Pick Up Drop Off Location: Transport by: Time:	Pick Up Drop Off Location: Transport by: Time:	Pick Up Drop Off Location: Transport by: Time:	Pick Up Drop Off Location: Transport by: Time:	Pick Up Drop Off Location: Transport by: Time:	Pick Up Drop Off Location: Transport by: Time:	Hours ___
C V								
	Pick Up Drop Off Location: Transport by: Time:	Pick Up Drop Off Location: Transport by: Time:	Pick Up Drop Off Location: Transport by: Time:	Pick Up. Drop Off Location: Transport by: Time:	Pick Up Drop Off Location: Transport by: Time:	Pick Up Drop Off. Location: Transport by: Time:	Pick Up Drop Off Location: Transport by: Time:	Hours ___
C V								
	Pick Up Drop Off Location: Transport by: Time:	Pick Up Drop Off Location: Transport by: Time:	Pick Up Drop Off Location: Transport by: Time:	Pick Up Drop Off Location: Transport by: Time:	Pick Up Drop Off Location: Transport by: Time:	Pick Up Drop Off Location: Transport by: Time:	Pick Up Drop Off Location: Transport by: Time:	Hours ___
C V								
	Pick Up Drop Off Location: Transport by: Time:	Pick Up Drop Off Location: Transport by: Time:	Pick Up Drop Off Location: Transport by: Time:	Pick Up Drop Off Location: Transport by: Time:	Pick Up Drop Off Location: Transport by: Time:	Pick Up Drop Off Location: Transport by: Time:	Pick Up Drop Off Location: Transport by: Time:	Hours ___
C V								

Monthly Total _____ **Custody** _____ **Visitation** _____ **Hours**

Hours by Month and Week

January has 31 days = 744 hours
February has 28 or 29 days = 672 or 696 hours
March has 31 days = 744 hours
April has 30 days = 720 hours
May has 31 days = 744 hours
June has 30 days = 720 hours
July has 31 days = 744 hours
August has 31 days = 744 hours
September has 30 days = 720 hours
October has 31 days = 744 hours
November has 30 days = 720 hours
December has 31 days = 744 hours

1 Day Week = 24 Hours
2 Day Week = 48 Hours
3 Day Week = 72 Hours
4 Day Week = 96 Hours
5 Day Week = 120 Hours
6 Day Week = 144 Hours
7 Day Week = 168 Hours

Calculate the Visitation Percentage:

_____ Visitation Hours ÷ _____ Total Hours in Month = _____ X 100 = _____ Visitation %

Calculate the Custody Percentage:

_____ Custody Hours ÷ _____ Total Hours in Month = _____ X 100 = _____ Custody %

Example: 144 Visitation Hours ÷ 744 Total Hours in July = .19 x 100 = 19% Visitation Percentage

Number of Overnights:	Secondary Household Total **Visitation**:	Primary Household Total **Custody**:

Month/Year: _____

	SU	M	T	W	TH	F	SA	
	Pick Up. Drop Off Location: Transport by: Time:	Pick Up Drop Off Location: Transport by: Time:	Pick Up Drop Off Location: Transport by: Time:	Pick Up Drop Off Location: Transport by: Time:	Pick Up Drop Off Location: Transport by: Time:	Pick Up Drop Off Location: Transport by: Time:	Pick Up Drop Off Location: Transport by: Time:	Hours
C V								
	Pick Up Drop Off Location: Transport by: Time:	Pick Up Drop Off Location: Transport by: Time:	Pick Up Drop Off Location: Transport by: Time:	Pick Up Drop Off Location: Transport by: Time:	Pick Up Drop Off Location: Transport by: Time:	Pick Up. Drop Off. Location: Transport by: Time:	Pick Up Drop Off Location: Transport by: Time:	Hours
C V								
	Pick Up. X Drop Off Location: house Transport by: Dad Time: 1 p.m.	Pick Up Drop Off Location: Transport by: Time:	Pick Up Drop Off Location: Transport by: Time:	Pick Up Drop Off Location: Transport by: Time:	Pick Up Drop Off Location: Transport by: Time:	Pick Up Drop Off Location: Transport by: Time:	Pick Up Drop Off Location: Transport by: Time:	Hours
C V								
	Pick Up Drop Off Location: Transport by: Time:	Pick Up Drop Off Location: Transport by: Time:	Pick Up Drop Off Location: Transport by: Time:	Pick Up. Drop Off Location: Transport by: Time:	Pick Up Drop Off Location: Transport by: Time:	Pick Up Drop Off. Location: Transport by: Time:	Pick Up Drop Off Location: Transport by: Time:	Hours
C V								
	Pick Up Drop Off Location: Transport by: Time:	Pick Up Drop Off Location: Transport by: Time:	Pick Up Drop Off Location: Transport by: Time:	Pick Up Drop Off Location: Transport by: Time:	Pick Up Drop Off Location: Transport by: Time:	Pick Up Drop Off Location: Transport by: Time:	Pick Up Drop Off Location: Transport by: Time:	Hours
C V								
	Pick Up Drop Off Location: Transport by: Time:	Pick Up Drop Off Location: Transport by: Time:	Pick Up Drop Off Location: Transport by: Time:	Pick Up Drop Off Location: Transport by: Time:	Pick Up Drop Off Location: Transport by: Time:	Pick Up Drop Off Location: Transport by: Time:	Pick Up Drop Off Location: Transport by: Time:	Hours
C V								

Monthly Total _____ **Custody** _____ **Visitation** _____ **Hours**

Hours by Month and Week

January has 31 days = 744 hours
February has 28 or 29 days = 672 or 696 hours
March has 31 days = 744 hours
April has 30 days = 720 hours
May has 31 days = 744 hours
June has 30 days = 720 hours
July has 31 days = 744 hours
August has 31 days = 744 hours
September has 30 days = 720 hours
October has 31 days = 744 hours
November has 30 days = 720 hours
December has 31 days = 744 hours

1 Day Week = 24 Hours
2 Day Week = 48 Hours
3 Day Week = 72 Hours
4 Day Week = 96 Hours
5 Day Week = 120 Hours
6 Day Week = 144 Hours
7 Day Week = 168 Hours

Calculate the Visitation Percentage:

_____ Visitation Hours ÷ _____ Total Hours in Month = _____ X 100 = _____ Visitation %

Calculate the Custody Percentage:

_____ Custody Hours ÷ _____ Total Hours in Month = _____ X 100 = _____ Custody %

Example: 144 Visitation Hours ÷ 744 Total Hours in July = .19 x 100 = 19% Visitation Percentage

Number of Overnights:	Secondary Household Total **Visitation**:	Primary Household Total **Custody**:

Month/Year: _____

	SU	M	T	W	TH	F	SA	
	Pick Up. Drop Off Location: Transport by: Time:	Pick Up Drop Off Location: Transport by: Time:	Pick Up Drop Off Location: Transport by: Time:	Pick Up Drop Off Location: Transport by: Time:	Pick Up Drop Off Location: Transport by: Time:	Pick Up Drop Off Location: Transport by: Time:	Pick Up Drop Off Location: Transport by: Time:	Hours
C **V**								/
	Pick Up Drop Off Location: Transport by: Time:	Pick Up Drop Off Location: Transport by: Time:	Pick Up Drop Off Location: Transport by: Time:	Pick Up Drop Off Location: Transport by: Time:	Pick Up Drop Off Location: Transport by: Time:	Pick Up. Drop Off. Location: Transport by: Time:	Pick Up Drop Off Location: Transport by: Time:	Hours
C **V**								/
	Pick Up. X Drop Off Location: house Transport by: Dad Time: 1 p.m.	Pick Up Drop Off Location: Transport by: Time:	Pick Up Drop Off Location: Transport by: Time:	Pick Up Drop Off Location: Transport by: Time:	Pick Up Drop Off Location: Transport by: Time:	Pick Up Drop Off Location: Transport by: Time:	Pick Up Drop Off Location: Transport by: Time:	Hours
C **V**								/
	Pick Up Drop Off Location: Transport by: Time:	Pick Up Drop Off Location: Transport by: Time:	Pick Up Drop Off Location: Transport by: Time:	Pick Up. Drop Off Location: Transport by: Time:	Pick Up Drop Off Location: Transport by: Time:	Pick Up Drop Off. Location: Transport by: Time:	Pick Up Drop Off Location: Transport by: Time:	Hours
C **V**								/
	Pick Up Drop Off Location: Transport by: Time:	Pick Up Drop Off Location: Transport by: Time:	Pick Up Drop Off Location: Transport by: Time:	Pick Up Drop Off Location: Transport by: Time:	Pick Up Drop Off Location: Transport by: Time:	Pick Up Drop Off Location: Transport by: Time:	Pick Up Drop Off Location: Transport by: Time:	Hours
C **V**								/
	Pick Up Drop Off Location: Transport by: Time:	Pick Up Drop Off Location: Transport by: Time:	Pick Up Drop Off Location: Transport by: Time:	Pick Up Drop Off Location: Transport by: Time:	Pick Up Drop Off Location: Transport by: Time:	Pick Up Drop Off Location: Transport by: Time:	Pick Up Drop Off Location: Transport by: Time:	Hours
C **V**								/

Monthly Total _____   **Custody** _____   **Visitation** _____ **Hours**

Hours by Month and Week

January has 31 days = 744 hours
February has 28 or 29 days = 672 or 696 hours
March has 31 days = 744 hours
April has 30 days = 720 hours
May has 31 days = 744 hours
June has 30 days = 720 hours
July has 31 days = 744 hours
August has 31 days = 744 hours
September has 30 days = 720 hours
October has 31 days = 744 hours
November has 30 days = 720 hours
December has 31 days = 744 hours

1 Day Week = 24 Hours
2 Day Week = 48 Hours
3 Day Week = 72 Hours
4 Day Week = 96 Hours
5 Day Week = 120 Hours
6 Day Week = 144 Hours
7 Day Week = 168 Hours

Calculate the Visitation Percentage:

_____ Visitation Hours ÷ _____ Total Hours in Month = _____ X 100 = _____ Visitation %

Calculate the Custody Percentage:

_____ Custody Hours ÷ _____ Total Hours in Month = _____ X 100 = _____ Custody %

Example: 144 Visitation Hours ÷ 744 Total Hours in July = .19 x 100 = 19% Visitation Percentage

Number of Overnights:	Secondary Household Total **Visitation**:	Primary Household Total **Custody**:

Month/Year:_____

Custody / Visitation Schedule

	SU	M	T	W	TH	F	SA	
C **V**	Pick Up. Drop Off Location: Transport by: Time:	Pick Up Drop Off Location: Transport by: Time:	Pick Up Drop Off Location: Transport by: Time:	Pick Up Drop Off Location: Transport by: Time:	Pick Up Drop Off Location: Transport by: Time:	Pick Up Drop Off Location: Transport by: Time:	Pick Up Drop Off Location: Transport by: Time:	Hours ___/___
C **V**	Pick Up Drop Off Location: Transport by: Time:	Pick Up Drop Off Location: Transport by: Time:	Pick Up Drop Off Location: Transport by: Time:	Pick Up Drop Off Location: Transport by: Time:	Pick Up Drop Off Location: Transport by: Time:	Pick Up. Drop Off. Location: Transport by: Time:	Pick Up Drop Off Location: Transport by: Time:	Hours ___/___
C **V**	Pick Up. X Drop Off Location: house Transport by: Dad Time: 1 p.m.	Pick Up Drop Off Location: Transport by: Time:	Pick Up Drop Off Location: Transport by: Time:	Pick Up Drop Off Location: Transport by: Time:	Pick Up Drop Off Location: Transport by: Time:	Pick Up Drop Off Location: Transport by: Time:	Pick Up Drop Off Location: Transport by: Time:	Hours ___/___
C **V**	Pick Up Drop Off Location: Transport by: Time:	Pick Up Drop Off Location: Transport by: Time:	Pick Up Drop Off Location: Transport by: Time:	Pick Up. Drop Off Location: Transport by: Time:	Pick Up Drop Off Location: Transport by: Time:	Pick Up Drop Off. Location: Transport by: Time:	Pick Up Drop Off Location: Transport by: Time:	Hours ___/___
C **V**	Pick Up Drop Off Location: Transport by: Time:	Pick Up Drop Off Location: Transport by: Time:	Pick Up Drop Off Location: Transport by: Time:	Pick Up Drop Off Location: Transport by: Time:	Pick Up Drop Off Location: Transport by: Time:	Pick Up Drop Off Location: Transport by: Time:	Pick Up Drop Off Location: Transport by: Time:	Hours ___/___
C **V**	Pick Up Drop Off Location: Transport by: Time:	Pick Up Drop Off Location: Transport by: Time:	Pick Up Drop Off Location: Transport by: Time:	Pick Up Drop Off Location: Transport by: Time:	Pick Up Drop Off Location: Transport by: Time:	Pick Up Drop Off Location: Transport by: Time:	Pick Up Drop Off Location: Transport by: Time:	Hours ___/___

Monthly Total _____   **Custody** _____   **Visitation** _____   **Hours**

Hours by Month and Week

January has 31 days = 744 hours
February has 28 or 29 days = 672 or 696 hours
March has 31 days = 744 hours
April has 30 days = 720 hours
May has 31 days = 744 hours
June has 30 days = 720 hours
July has 31 days = 744 hours
August has 31 days = 744 hours
September has 30 days = 720 hours
October has 31 days = 744 hours
November has 30 days = 720 hours
December has 31 days = 744 hours

1 Day Week = 24 Hours
2 Day Week = 48 Hours
3 Day Week = 72 Hours
4 Day Week = 96 Hours
5 Day Week = 120 Hours
6 Day Week = 144 Hours
7 Day Week = 168 Hours

Calculate the Visitation Percentage:

_____ Visitation Hours ÷ _____ Total Hours in Month = _____ X 100 = _____ Visitation %

Calculate the Custody Percentage:

_____ Custody Hours ÷ _____ Total Hours in Month = _____ X 100 = _____ Custody %

Example: 144 Visitation Hours ÷ 744 Total Hours in July = .19 x 100 = 19% Visitation Percentage

Number of Overnights:	Secondary Household Total **Visitation**:	Primary Household Total **Custody**:

Month/Year: _____

Custody / Visitation Schedule

	SU	M	T	W	TH	F	SA	
	Pick Up. Drop Off Location: Transport by: Time:	Pick Up Drop Off Location: Transport by: Time:	Pick Up Drop Off Location: Transport by: Time:	Pick Up Drop Off Location: Transport by: Time:	Pick Up Drop Off Location: Transport by: Time:	Pick Up Drop Off Location: Transport by: Time:	Pick Up Drop Off Location: Transport by: Time:	Hours ___ / ___
C **V**								
	Pick Up Drop Off Location: Transport by: Time:	Pick Up Drop Off Location: Transport by: Time:	Pick Up Drop Off Location: Transport by: Time:	Pick Up Drop Off Location: Transport by: Time:	Pick Up Drop Off Location: Transport by: Time:	Pick Up. Drop Off. Location: Transport by: Time:	Pick Up Drop Off Location: Transport by: Time:	Hours ___ / ___
C **V**								
	Pick Up. X Drop Off Location: house Transport by: Dad Time: 1 p.m.	Pick Up Drop Off Location: Transport by: Time:	Pick Up Drop Off Location: Transport by: Time:	Pick Up Drop Off Location: Transport by: Time:	Pick Up Drop Off Location: Transport by: Time:	Pick Up Drop Off Location: Transport by: Time:	Pick Up Drop Off Location: Transport by: Time:	Hours ___ / ___
C **V**								
	Pick Up Drop Off Location: Transport by: Time:	Pick Up Drop Off Location: Transport by: Time:	Pick Up Drop Off Location: Transport by: Time:	Pick Up. Drop Off Location: Transport by: Time:	Pick Up Drop Off Location: Transport by: Time:	Pick Up Drop Off. Location: Transport by: Time:	Pick Up Drop Off Location: Transport by: Time:	Hours ___ / ___
C **V**								
	Pick Up Drop Off Location: Transport by: Time:	Pick Up Drop Off Location: Transport by: Time:	Pick Up Drop Off Location: Transport by: Time:	Pick Up Drop Off Location: Transport by: Time:	Pick Up Drop Off Location: Transport by: Time:	Pick Up Drop Off Location: Transport by: Time:	Pick Up Drop Off Location: Transport by: Time:	Hours ___ / ___
C **V**								
	Pick Up Drop Off Location: Transport by: Time:	Pick Up Drop Off Location: Transport by: Time:	Pick Up Drop Off Location: Transport by: Time:	Pick Up Drop Off Location: Transport by: Time:	Pick Up Drop Off Location: Transport by: Time:	Pick Up Drop Off Location: Transport by: Time:	Pick Up Drop Off Location: Transport by: Time:	Hours ___ / ___
C **V**								

Monthly Total _____   **Custody** _____   **Visitation** _____ **Hours**

Hours by Month and Week

January has 31 days = 744 hours
February has 28 or 29 days = 672 or 696 hours
March has 31 days = 744 hours
April has 30 days = 720 hours
May has 31 days = 744 hours
June has 30 days = 720 hours
July has 31 days = 744 hours
August has 31 days = 744 hours
September has 30 days = 720 hours
October has 31 days = 744 hours
November has 30 days = 720 hours
December has 31 days = 744 hours

1 Day Week = 24 Hours
2 Day Week = 48 Hours
3 Day Week = 72 Hours
4 Day Week = 96 Hours
5 Day Week = 120 Hours
6 Day Week = 144 Hours
7 Day Week = 168 Hours

Calculate the Visitation Percentage:

_____ Visitation Hours ÷ _____ Total Hours in Month = _____ X 100 = _____ Visitation %

Calculate the Custody Percentage:

_____ Custody Hours ÷ _____ Total Hours in Month = _____ X 100 = _____ Custody %

Example: 144 Visitation Hours ÷ 744 Total Hours in July = .19 x 100 = 19% Visitation Percentage

Number of Overnights:	Secondary Household Total **Visitation**:	Primary Household Total **Custody**:

Month/Year: _____

	SU	M	T	W	TH	F	SA	Hours
C **V**	Pick Up. Drop Off Location: Transport by: Time:	Pick Up Drop Off Location: Transport by: Time:	Pick Up Drop Off Location: Transport by: Time:	Pick Up Drop Off Location: Transport by: Time:	Pick Up Drop Off Location: Transport by: Time:	Pick Up Drop Off Location: Transport by: Time:	Pick Up Drop Off Location: Transport by: Time:	Hours /
C **V**	Pick Up Drop Off Location: Transport by: Time:	Pick Up Drop Off Location: Transport by: Time:	Pick Up Drop Off Location: Transport by: Time:	Pick Up Drop Off Location: Transport by: Time:	Pick Up Drop Off Location: Transport by: Time:	Pick Up. Drop Off. Location: Transport by: Time:	Pick Up Drop Off Location: Transport by: Time:	Hours /
C **V**	Pick Up. X Drop Off Location: house Transport by: Dad Time: 1 p.m.	Pick Up Drop Off Location: Transport by: Time:	Pick Up Drop Off Location: Transport by: Time:	Pick Up Drop Off Location: Transport by: Time:	Pick Up Drop Off Location: Transport by: Time:	Pick Up Drop Off Location: Transport by: Time:	Pick Up Drop Off Location: Transport by: Time:	Hours /
C **V**	Pick Up Drop Off Location: Transport by: Time:	Pick Up Drop Off Location: Transport by: Time:	Pick Up Drop Off Location: Transport by: Time:	Pick Up. Drop Off Location: Transport by: Time:	Pick Up Drop Off Location: Transport by: Time:	Pick Up Drop Off. Location: Transport by: Time:	Pick Up Drop Off Location: Transport by: Time:	Hours /
C **V**	Pick Up Drop Off Location: Transport by: Time:	Pick Up Drop Off Location: Transport by: Time:	Pick Up Drop Off Location: Transport by: Time:	Pick Up Drop Off Location: Transport by: Time:	Pick Up Drop Off Location: Transport by: Time:	Pick Up Drop Off Location: Transport by: Time:	Pick Up Drop Off Location: Transport by: Time:	Hours /
C **V**	Pick Up Drop Off Location: Transport by: Time:	Pick Up Drop Off Location: Transport by: Time:	Pick Up Drop Off Location: Transport by: Time:	Pick Up Drop Off Location: Transport by: Time:	Pick Up Drop Off Location: Transport by: Time:	Pick Up Drop Off Location: Transport by: Time:	Pick Up Drop Off Location: Transport by: Time:	Hours /

Monthly Total _____   **Custody** _____   **Visitation** _____   **Hours**

Notes

Personal Calendars

Date:_____

SU	M	T	W	TH	F	SA

Date:_____

SU	M	T	W	TH	F	SA

Date:_____

SU	M	T	W	TH	F	SA

Date:_____

SU	M	T	W	TH	F	SA

Date:_____

SU	M	T	W	TH	F	SA

Date:_____

SU	M	T	W	TH	F	SA

Date:_____

SU	M	T	W	TH	F	SA

Date:_____

SU	M	T	W	TH	F	SA

Date:_____

SU	M	T	W	TH	F	SA

Date:_____

SU	M	T	W	TH	F	SA

Date:_____

SU	M	T	W	TH	F	SA

Date:_____

SU	M	T	W	TH	F	SA

Date:_____

SU	M	T	W	TH	F	SA

Date:_____

Personal Schedule

SU	M	T	W	TH	F	SA

Date: _____

SU	M	T	W	TH	F	SA

Date:_____

Personal Schedule

SU	M	T	W	TH	F	SA

Date:_____

SU	M	T	W	TH	F	SA

Child Support

Ledger

Date	Child Support Details					New Amount Due	−	Paid	=	Balance Due	Total Support Due
Previous Balance											15
8/8/19	Sample Payment 1 - Details	X	Scheduled	X	Payment	500	—	439	=	61	15
			Arrears		Interest						+ 61
9/01/19	Sample Payment 2 - Details		Scheduled	X	Payment	0	—	50	=	-50	= 76
		X	Arrears		Interest						+ -50
9/25/19	Sample Payment 3 - Details	X	Scheduled	X	Payment	150	—	35	=	115	= 26
			Arrears		Interest						+ 115
9/29/19	Sample Interest - Transaction 4		Scheduled		Payment	7	—	0	=	7	= 141
			Arrears	X	Interest						+ 7
								Remaining Child Support to be Paid		=	148

Example!

next page!

Figure Out Your "Balance Due"

Work the row from left to right.

Using the example above, carry your "Previous Balance" to the top space of the "Total Support Due" column.

15 —-> 15

Calculate your "**Balance Due**" by subtracting the "**Paid**" from the "**New** Amount Due."

$500.00 (*New* Amount Due) – **$439.00** (*Paid*) = **$61.00** (*Balance Due*) for Sample Payment 1
0.00 – $50.00 = (–$50.00) for Sample Payment 2.
$150.00 – $35.00 = $115.00 for Sample Payment 3
$7.00 - $0.00 = $7.00 for Interest Transaction 4

A positive figure in "Balance Due" indicates additional "Total Support Due."
A negative figure in "Remaining Balance Due" is a credit against the "Total Support Due."

Calculate your "Total Support Due" Column

Work the column from the top to the bottom.

Write the "Balance Due" figure in the designated space, see arrows above.
$61.00 —-> $61.00 (Sample 1)
(–$50.00) —-> (–$50.00) (Sample 2)
$115.00 —-> $115.00 (Sample 3)
$7.00 —-> $7.00 (Sample Interest 4)**

Calculate "**Total Support Due**" by adding the "Balance Due" and Previous Balance.
$15.00 + $61.00 = $76.00 (Sample 1)
76.00 + (– $50.00) = $26.00 (Sample 2)
$26.00 + $115.00 = $141.00 (Sample 3)
$141.00 + $7.00 = $148.00 (Sample 4)

This worksheet example shows $148.00 in "Remaining Child Support to be Paid."

**Each state calculates interest on arrears child support differently.
Look online for child support interest calculators or ask a professional.

Year: _____

 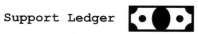

Date	Child Support Details			New Amount Due	_	Paid	=	Balance Due	Total Support Due
Previous Balance									
		Scheduled	Payment	—		=			
		Arrears	Interest						
		Scheduled	Payment	—		=			
		Arrears	Interest						
		Scheduled	Payment	—		=			
		Arrears	Interest						
		Scheduled	Payment	—		=			
		Arrears	Interest						
		Scheduled	Payment	—		=			
		Arrears	Interest						
		Scheduled	Payment	—		=			
		Arrears	Interest						
		Scheduled	Payment	—		=			
		Arrears	Interest						
		Scheduled	Payment	—		=			
		Arrears	Interest						
		Scheduled	Payment	—		=			
		Arrears	Interest						
		Scheduled	Payment	—		=			
		Arrears	Interest						
		Scheduled	Payment	—		=			
		Arrears	Interest						
		Scheduled	Payment	—		=			
		Arrears	Interest						
		Scheduled	Payment	—		=			
		Arrears	Interest						
		Scheduled	Payment	—		=			
		Arrears	Interest						
		Scheduled	Payment	—		=			
		Arrears	Interest						
		Scheduled	Payment	—		=			
		Arrears	Interest						
		Scheduled	Payment	—		=			
		Arrears	Interest						
					Remaining Child Support to be Paid				

Year: _____

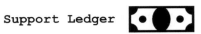

Date	Child Support Details			New Amount Due	−	Paid	=	Balance Due	Total Support Due
Previous Balance									
		Scheduled	Payment		—		=		
		Arrears	Interest						
		Scheduled	Payment		—		=		
		Arrears	Interest						
		Scheduled	Payment		—		=		
		Arrears	Interest						
		Scheduled	Payment		—		=		
		Arrears	Interest						
		Scheduled	Payment		—		=		
		Arrears	Interest						
		Scheduled	Payment		—		=		
		Arrears	Interest						
		Scheduled	Payment		—		=		
		Arrears	Interest						
		Scheduled	Payment		—		=		
		Arrears	Interest						
		Scheduled	Payment		—		=		
		Arrears	Interest						
		Scheduled	Payment		—		=		
		Arrears	Interest						
		Scheduled	Payment		—		=		
		Arrears	Interest						
		Scheduled	Payment		—		=		
		Arrears	Interest						
		Scheduled	Payment		—		=		
		Arrears	Interest						
		Scheduled	Payment		—		=		
		Arrears	Interest						
		Scheduled	Payment		—		=		
		Arrears	Interest						
		Scheduled	Payment		—		=		
		Arrears	Interest						
		Scheduled	Payment		—		=		
		Arrears	Interest						
						Remaining Child Support to be Paid			

Year: _____

Date	Child Support Details			New Amount Due	−	Paid	=	Balance Due	Total Support Due
Previous Balance									
		Scheduled	Payment	—		=			
		Arrears	Interest						
		Scheduled	Payment	—		=			
		Arrears	Interest						
		Scheduled	Payment	—		=			
		Arrears	Interest						
		Scheduled	Payment	—		=			
		Arrears	Interest						
		Scheduled	Payment	—		=			
		Arrears	Interest						
		Scheduled	Payment	—		=			
		Arrears	Interest						
		Scheduled	Payment	—		=			
		Arrears	Interest						
		Scheduled	Payment	—		=			
		Arrears	Interest						
		Scheduled	Payment	—		=			
		Arrears	Interest						
		Scheduled	Payment	—		=			
		Arrears	Interest						
		Scheduled	Payment	—		=			
		Arrears	Interest						
		Scheduled	Payment	—		=			
		Arrears	Interest						
		Scheduled	Payment	—		=			
		Arrears	Interest						
		Scheduled	Payment	—		=			
		Arrears	Interest						
		Scheduled	Payment	—		=			
		Arrears	Interest						
		Scheduled	Payment	—		=			
		Arrears	Interest						
		Scheduled	Payment	—		=			
		Arrears	Interest						
						Remaining Child Support to be Paid			

Year: _____

 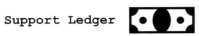

Date	Child Support Details			New Amount Due	–	Paid	=	Balance Due	Total Support Due
Previous Balance									
		Scheduled	Payment	—		=			
		Arrears	Interest						
		Scheduled	Payment	—		=			
		Arrears	Interest						
		Scheduled	Payment	—		=			
		Arrears	Interest						
		Scheduled	Payment	—		=			
		Arrears	Interest						
		Scheduled	Payment	—		=			
		Arrears	Interest						
		Scheduled	Payment	—		=			
		Arrears	Interest						
		Scheduled	Payment	—		=			
		Arrears	Interest						
		Scheduled	Payment	—		=			
		Arrears	Interest						
		Scheduled	Payment	—		=			
		Arrears	Interest						
		Scheduled	Payment	—		=			
		Arrears	Interest						
		Scheduled	Payment	—		=			
		Arrears	Interest						
		Scheduled	Payment	—		=			
		Arrears	Interest						
		Scheduled	Payment	—		=			
		Arrears	Interest						
		Scheduled	Payment	—		=			
		Arrears	Interest						
		Scheduled	Payment	—		=			
		Arrears	Interest						
		Scheduled	Payment	—		=			
		Arrears	Interest						
		Scheduled	Payment	—		=			
		Arrears	Interest						
Remaining Child Support to be Paid									

Year: _____

 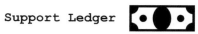

Date	Child Support Details			New Amount Due	−	Paid	=	Balance Due	Total Support Due
Previous Balance									
		Scheduled	Payment		—		=		
		Arrears	Interest						
		Scheduled	Payment		—		=		
		Arrears	Interest						
		Scheduled	Payment		—		=		
		Arrears	Interest						
		Scheduled	Payment		—		=		
		Arrears	Interest						
		Scheduled	Payment		—		=		
		Arrears	Interest						
		Scheduled	Payment		—		=		
		Arrears	Interest						
		Scheduled	Payment		—		=		
		Arrears	Interest						
		Scheduled	Payment		—		=		
		Arrears	Interest						
		Scheduled	Payment		—		=		
		Arrears	Interest						
		Scheduled	Payment		—		=		
		Arrears	Interest						
		Scheduled	Payment		—		=		
		Arrears	Interest						
		Scheduled	Payment		—		=		
		Arrears	Interest						
		Scheduled	Payment		—		=		
		Arrears	Interest						
		Scheduled	Payment		—		=		
		Arrears	Interest						
		Scheduled	Payment		—		=		
		Arrears	Interest						
		Scheduled	Payment		—		=		
		Arrears	Interest						
		Scheduled	Payment		—		=		
		Arrears	Interest						
					Remaining Child Support to be Paid				

Year: _____

 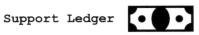

Date	Child Support Details					New Amount Due	−	Paid	=	Balance Due	Total Support Due
Previous Balance											
			Scheduled		Payment	—			=		
			Arrears		Interest						
			Scheduled		Payment	—			=		
			Arrears		Interest						
			Scheduled		Payment	—			=		
			Arrears		Interest						
			Scheduled		Payment	—			=		
			Arrears		Interest						
			Scheduled		Payment	—			=		
			Arrears		Interest						
			Scheduled		Payment	—			=		
			Arrears		Interest						
			Scheduled		Payment	—			=		
			Arrears		Interest						
			Scheduled		Payment	—			=		
			Arrears		Interest						
			Scheduled		Payment	—			=		
			Arrears		Interest						
			Scheduled		Payment	—			=		
			Arrears		Interest						
			Scheduled		Payment	—			=		
			Arrears		Interest						
			Scheduled		Payment	—			=		
			Arrears		Interest						
			Scheduled		Payment	—			=		
			Arrears		Interest						
			Scheduled		Payment	—			=		
			Arrears		Interest						
			Scheduled		Payment	—			=		
			Arrears		Interest						
			Scheduled		Payment	—			=		
			Arrears		Interest						
			Scheduled		Payment	—			=		
			Arrears		Interest						
							Remaining Child Support to be Paid				

Year: _____

 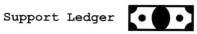

Date	Child Support Details			New Amount Due	−	Paid	=	Balance Due	Total Support Due
Previous Balance									
		Scheduled	Payment		—		=		
		Arrears	Interest						
		Scheduled	Payment		—		=		
		Arrears	Interest						
		Scheduled	Payment		—		=		
		Arrears	Interest						
		Scheduled	Payment		—		=		
		Arrears	Interest						
		Scheduled	Payment		—		=		
		Arrears	Interest						
		Scheduled	Payment		—		=		
		Arrears	Interest						
		Scheduled	Payment		—		=		
		Arrears	Interest						
		Scheduled	Payment		—		=		
		Arrears	Interest						
		Scheduled	Payment		—		=		
		Arrears	Interest						
		Scheduled	Payment		—		=		
		Arrears	Interest						
		Scheduled	Payment		—		=		
		Arrears	Interest						
		Scheduled	Payment		—		=		
		Arrears	Interest						
		Scheduled	Payment		—		=		
		Arrears	Interest						
		Scheduled	Payment		—		=		
		Arrears	Interest						
		Scheduled	Payment		—		=		
		Arrears	Interest						
		Scheduled	Payment		—		=		
		Arrears	Interest						
		Scheduled	Payment		—		=		
		Arrears	Interest						
					Remaining Child Support to be Paid				

Year: _____

 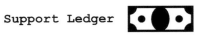

Date	Child Support Details			New Amount Due	_	Paid	=	Balance Due	Total Support Due
Previous Balance									
		Scheduled	Payment	—		=			
		Arrears	Interest						
		Scheduled	Payment	—		=			
		Arrears	Interest						
		Scheduled	Payment	—		=			
		Arrears	Interest						
		Scheduled	Payment	—		=			
		Arrears	Interest						
		Scheduled	Payment	—		=			
		Arrears	Interest						
		Scheduled	Payment	—		=			
		Arrears	Interest						
		Scheduled	Payment	—		=			
		Arrears	Interest						
		Scheduled	Payment	—		=			
		Arrears	Interest						
		Scheduled	Payment	—		=			
		Arrears	Interest						
		Scheduled	Payment	—		=			
		Arrears	Interest						
		Scheduled	Payment	—		=			
		Arrears	Interest						
		Scheduled	Payment	—		=			
		Arrears	Interest						
		Scheduled	Payment	—		=			
		Arrears	Interest						
		Scheduled	Payment	—		=			
		Arrears	Interest						
		Scheduled	Payment	—		=			
		Arrears	Interest						
		Scheduled	Payment	—		=			
		Arrears	Interest						
		Scheduled	Payment	—		=			
		Arrears	Interest						
					Remaining Child Support to be Paid				

Year: _____

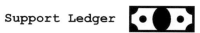

Support Ledger

Date	Child Support Details			New Amount Due	_	Paid	=	Balance Due	Total Support Due
Previous Balance									
		☐ Scheduled ☐ Arrears	☐ Payment ☐ Interest	—			=		
		☐ Scheduled ☐ Arrears	☐ Payment ☐ Interest	—			=		
		☐ Scheduled ☐ Arrears	☐ Payment ☐ Interest	—			=		
		☐ Scheduled ☐ Arrears	☐ Payment ☐ Interest	—			=		
		☐ Scheduled ☐ Arrears	☐ Payment ☐ Interest	—			=		
		☐ Scheduled ☐ Arrears	☐ Payment ☐ Interest	—			=		
		☐ Scheduled ☐ Arrears	☐ Payment ☐ Interest	—			=		
		☐ Scheduled ☐ Arrears	☐ Payment ☐ Interest	—			=		
		☐ Scheduled ☐ Arrears	☐ Payment ☐ Interest	—			=		
		☐ Scheduled ☐ Arrears	☐ Payment ☐ Interest	—			=		
		☐ Scheduled ☐ Arrears	☐ Payment ☐ Interest	—			=		
		☐ Scheduled ☐ Arrears	☐ Payment ☐ Interest	—			=		
		☐ Scheduled ☐ Arrears	☐ Payment ☐ Interest	—			=		
		☐ Scheduled ☐ Arrears	☐ Payment ☐ Interest	—			=		
		☐ Scheduled ☐ Arrears	☐ Payment ☐ Interest	—			=		
		☐ Scheduled ☐ Arrears	☐ Payment ☐ Interest	—			=		
		☐ Scheduled ☐ Arrears	☐ Payment ☐ Interest	—			=		
				Remaining Child Support to be Paid					

Year: _____

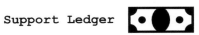

Date	Child Support Details			New Amount Due	_	Paid	=	Balance Due	Total Support Due
Previous Balance									
		Scheduled	Payment		—		=		
		Arrears	Interest						
		Scheduled	Payment		—		=		
		Arrears	Interest						
		Scheduled	Payment		—		=		
		Arrears	Interest						
		Scheduled	Payment		—		=		
		Arrears	Interest						
		Scheduled	Payment		—		=		
		Arrears	Interest						
		Scheduled	Payment		—		=		
		Arrears	Interest						
		Scheduled	Payment		—		=		
		Arrears	Interest						
		Scheduled	Payment		—		=		
		Arrears	Interest						
		Scheduled	Payment		—		=		
		Arrears	Interest						
		Scheduled	Payment		—		=		
		Arrears	Interest						
		Scheduled	Payment		—		=		
		Arrears	Interest						
		Scheduled	Payment		—		=		
		Arrears	Interest						
		Scheduled	Payment		—		=		
		Arrears	Interest						
		Scheduled	Payment		—		=		
		Arrears	Interest						
		Scheduled	Payment		—		=		
		Arrears	Interest						
		Scheduled	Payment		—		=		
		Arrears	Interest						
		Scheduled	Payment		—		=		
		Arrears	Interest						
Remaining Child Support to be Paid									

Year: _____

Date	Child Support Details			New Amount Due	–	Paid	=	Balance Due	Total Support Due
Previous Balance									
		Scheduled	Payment		—		=		
		Arrears	Interest						
		Scheduled	Payment		—		=		
		Arrears	Interest						
		Scheduled	Payment		—		=		
		Arrears	Interest						
		Scheduled	Payment		—		=		
		Arrears	Interest						
		Scheduled	Payment		—		=		
		Arrears	Interest						
		Scheduled	Payment		—		=		
		Arrears	Interest						
		Scheduled	Payment		—		=		
		Arrears	Interest						
		Scheduled	Payment		—		=		
		Arrears	Interest						
		Scheduled	Payment		—		=		
		Arrears	Interest						
		Scheduled	Payment		—		=		
		Arrears	Interest						
		Scheduled	Payment		—		=		
		Arrears	Interest						
		Scheduled	Payment		—		=		
		Arrears	Interest						
		Scheduled	Payment		—		=		
		Arrears	Interest						
		Scheduled	Payment		—		=		
		Arrears	Interest						
		Scheduled	Payment		—		=		
		Arrears	Interest						
		Scheduled	Payment		—		=		
		Arrears	Interest						
				Remaining Child Support to be Paid					

Year:_____

 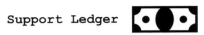

Date	Child Support Details				New Amount Due	_	Paid	=	Balance Due	Total Support Due
Previous Balance										
		Scheduled		Payment	—			=		
		Arrears		Interest						
		Scheduled		Payment	—			=		
		Arrears		Interest						
		Scheduled		Payment	—			=		
		Arrears		Interest						
		Scheduled		Payment	—			=		
		Arrears		Interest						
		Scheduled		Payment	—			=		
		Arrears		Interest						
		Scheduled		Payment	—			=		
		Arrears		Interest						
		Scheduled		Payment	—			=		
		Arrears		Interest						
		Scheduled		Payment	—			=		
		Arrears		Interest						
		Scheduled		Payment	—			=		
		Arrears		Interest						
		Scheduled		Payment	—			=		
		Arrears		Interest						
		Scheduled		Payment	—			=		
		Arrears		Interest						
		Scheduled		Payment	—			=		
		Arrears		Interest						
		Scheduled		Payment	—			=		
		Arrears		Interest						
		Scheduled		Payment	—			=		
		Arrears		Interest						
		Scheduled		Payment	—			=		
		Arrears		Interest						
		Scheduled		Payment	—			=		
		Arrears		Interest						
		Scheduled		Payment	—			=		
		Arrears		Interest						
						Remaining Child Support to be Paid				

Year: _____

 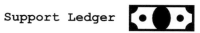

Date	Child Support Details			New Amount Due	−	Paid	=	Balance Due	Total Support Due
Previous Balance									
		Scheduled	Payment		—		=		
		Arrears	Interest						
		Scheduled	Payment		—		=		
		Arrears	Interest						
		Scheduled	Payment		—		=		
		Arrears	Interest						
		Scheduled	Payment		—		=		
		Arrears	Interest						
		Scheduled	Payment		—		=		
		Arrears	Interest						
		Scheduled	Payment		—		=		
		Arrears	Interest						
		Scheduled	Payment		—		=		
		Arrears	Interest						
		Scheduled	Payment		—		=		
		Arrears	Interest						
		Scheduled	Payment		—		=		
		Arrears	Interest						
		Scheduled	Payment		—		=		
		Arrears	Interest						
		Scheduled	Payment		—		=		
		Arrears	Interest						
		Scheduled	Payment		—		=		
		Arrears	Interest						
		Scheduled	Payment		—		=		
		Arrears	Interest						
		Scheduled	Payment		—		=		
		Arrears	Interest						
		Scheduled	Payment		—		=		
		Arrears	Interest						
		Scheduled	Payment		—		=		
		Arrears	Interest						
		Scheduled	Payment		—		=		
		Arrears	Interest						
						Remaining Child Support to be Paid			

Year: _____

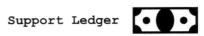

Support Ledger

Date	Child Support Details			New Amount Due	−	Paid	=	Balance Due	Total Support Due
Previous Balance									
		Scheduled Arrears	Payment Interest	—			=		
		Scheduled Arrears	Payment Interest	—			=		
		Scheduled Arrears	Payment Interest	—			=		
		Scheduled Arrears	Payment Interest	—			=		
		Scheduled Arrears	Payment Interest	—			=		
		Scheduled Arrears	Payment Interest	—			=		
		Scheduled Arrears	Payment Interest	—			=		
		Scheduled Arrears	Payment Interest	—			=		
		Scheduled Arrears	Payment Interest	—			=		
		Scheduled Arrears	Payment Interest	—			=		
		Scheduled Arrears	Payment Interest	—			=		
		Scheduled Arrears	Payment Interest	—			=		
		Scheduled Arrears	Payment Interest	—			=		
		Scheduled Arrears	Payment Interest	—			=		
		Scheduled Arrears	Payment Interest	—			=		
		Scheduled Arrears	Payment Interest	—			=		
		Scheduled Arrears	Payment Interest	—			=		
						Remaining Child Support to be Paid			

Year: _____

 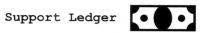

Date	Child Support Details			New Amount Due	_	Paid	=	Balance Due	Total Support Due
Previous Balance									
		Scheduled	Payment	—		=			
		Arrears	Interest						
		Scheduled	Payment	—		=			
		Arrears	Interest						
		Scheduled	Payment	—		=			
		Arrears	Interest						
		Scheduled	Payment	—		=			
		Arrears	Interest						
		Scheduled	Payment	—		=			
		Arrears	Interest						
		Scheduled	Payment	—		=			
		Arrears	Interest						
		Scheduled	Payment	—		=			
		Arrears	Interest						
		Scheduled	Payment	—		=			
		Arrears	Interest						
		Scheduled	Payment	—		=			
		Arrears	Interest						
		Scheduled	Payment	—		=			
		Arrears	Interest						
		Scheduled	Payment	—		=			
		Arrears	Interest						
		Scheduled	Payment	—		=			
		Arrears	Interest						
		Scheduled	Payment	—		=			
		Arrears	Interest						
		Scheduled	Payment	—		=			
		Arrears	Interest						
		Scheduled	Payment	—		=			
		Arrears	Interest						
		Scheduled	Payment	—		=			
		Arrears	Interest						
		Scheduled	Payment	—		=			
		Arrears	Interest						
				Remaining Child Support to be Paid					

Year: _____

 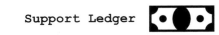

Date	Child Support Details			New Amount Due	−	Paid	=	Balance Due	Total Support Due
Previous Balance									
		Scheduled	Payment		—		=		
		Arrears	Interest						
		Scheduled	Payment		—		=		
		Arrears	Interest						
		Scheduled	Payment		—		=		
		Arrears	Interest						
		Scheduled	Payment		—		=		
		Arrears	Interest						
		Scheduled	Payment		—		=		
		Arrears	Interest						
		Scheduled	Payment		—		=		
		Arrears	Interest						
		Scheduled	Payment		—		=		
		Arrears	Interest						
		Scheduled	Payment		—		=		
		Arrears	Interest						
		Scheduled	Payment		—		=		
		Arrears	Interest						
		Scheduled	Payment		—		=		
		Arrears	Interest						
		Scheduled	Payment		—		=		
		Arrears	Interest						
		Scheduled	Payment		—		=		
		Arrears	Interest						
		Scheduled	Payment		—		=		
		Arrears	Interest						
		Scheduled	Payment		—		=		
		Arrears	Interest						
		Scheduled	Payment		—		=		
		Arrears	Interest						
		Scheduled	Payment		—		=		
		Arrears	Interest						
		Scheduled	Payment		—		=		
		Arrears	Interest						
					Remaining Child Support to be Paid					

Year: _____

 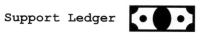

Date	Child Support Details				New Amount Due	−	Paid	=	Balance Due	Total Support Due
Previous Balance										
			Scheduled		Payment	—		=		....
			Arrears		Interest					
			Scheduled		Payment	—		=		....
			Arrears		Interest					
			Scheduled		Payment	—		=		....
			Arrears		Interest					
			Scheduled		Payment	—		=		....
			Arrears		Interest					
			Scheduled		Payment	—		=		....
			Arrears		Interest					
			Scheduled		Payment	—		=		....
			Arrears		Interest					
			Scheduled		Payment	—		=		....
			Arrears		Interest					
			Scheduled		Payment	—		=		....
			Arrears		Interest					
			Scheduled		Payment	—		=		....
			Arrears		Interest					
			Scheduled		Payment	—		=		....
			Arrears		Interest					
			Scheduled		Payment	—		=		....
			Arrears		Interest					
			Scheduled		Payment	—		=		....
			Arrears		Interest					
			Scheduled		Payment	—		=		....
			Arrears		Interest					
			Scheduled		Payment	—		=		....
			Arrears		Interest					
			Scheduled		Payment	—		=		....
			Arrears		Interest					
			Scheduled		Payment	—		=		....
			Arrears		Interest					
			Scheduled		Payment	—		=		....
			Arrears		Interest					
Remaining Child Support to be Paid										

Year: _____

 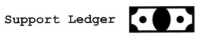

Date	Child Support Details			New Amount Due	_	Paid	=	Balance Due	Total Support Due
Previous Balance									
		Scheduled	Payment		—		=		
		Arrears	Interest						
		Scheduled	Payment		—		=		
		Arrears	Interest						
		Scheduled	Payment		—		=		
		Arrears	Interest						
		Scheduled	Payment		—		=		
		Arrears	Interest						
		Scheduled	Payment		—		=		
		Arrears	Interest						
		Scheduled	Payment		—		=		
		Arrears	Interest						
		Scheduled	Payment		—		=		
		Arrears	Interest						
		Scheduled	Payment		—		=		
		Arrears	Interest						
		Scheduled	Payment		—		=		
		Arrears	Interest						
		Scheduled	Payment		—		=		
		Arrears	Interest						
		Scheduled	Payment		—		=		
		Arrears	Interest						
		Scheduled	Payment		—		=		
		Arrears	Interest						
		Scheduled	Payment		—		=		
		Arrears	Interest						
		Scheduled	Payment		—		=		
		Arrears	Interest						
		Scheduled	Payment		—		=		
		Arrears	Interest						
		Scheduled	Payment		—		=		
		Arrears	Interest						
		Scheduled	Payment		—		=		
		Arrears	Interest						
						Remaining Child Support to be Paid			

Shared Expenses

Date:_____

 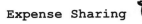

Date	Category	Description	My Payment Amount	% Reimburse	Other Parent Owes	Date Reimbursed	Notes
			$	%	$		
			$	%	$		
			$	%	$		
			$	%	$		
			$	%	$		
			$	%	$		
			$	%	$		
			$	%	$		
			$	%	$		
			$	%	$		
			$	%	$		
			$	%	$		
			$	%	$		
			$	%	$		
			$	%	$		
			$	%	$		
			$	%	$		
			$	%	$		
			$	%	$		
			$	%	$		
		TOTALS	$		$		

Date	Category	Description	Other Parent's Payment	% Reimburse	I Owe	Date I Reimbursed	Notes
			$	%	$		
			$	%	$		
			$	%	$		
			$	%	$		
			$	%	$		
			$	%	$		
			$	%	$		
			$	%	$		
			$	%	$		
			$	%	$		
		TOTALS	$		$		

Date:_____

Date	Category	Description	My Payment Amount	% Reimburse	Other Parent Owes	Date Reimbursed	Notes
			$	%	$		
			$	%	$		
			$	%	$		
			$	%	$		
			$	%	$		
			$	%	$		
			$	%	$		
			$	%	$		
			$	%	$		
			$	%	$		
			$	%	$		
			$	%	$		
			$	%	$		
			$	%	$		
			$	%	$		
			$	%	$		
			$	%	$		
			$	%	$		
			$	%	$		
			$	%	$		
		TOTALS	$		$		

Date	Category	Description	Other Parent's Payment	% Reimburse	I Owe	Date I Reimbursed	Notes
			$	%	$		
			$	%	$		
			$	%	$		
			$	%	$		
			$	%	$		
			$	%	$		
			$	%	$		
			$	%	$		
			$	%	$		
			$	%	$		
		TOTALS	$		$		

Date:_____

Date	Category	Description	My Payment Amount	% Reimburse	Other Parent Owes	Date Reimbursed	Notes
			$	%	$		
			$	%	$		
			$	%	$		
			$	%	$		
			$	%	$		
			$	%	$		
			$	%	$		
			$	%	$		
			$	%	$		
			$	%	$		
			$	%	$		
			$	%	$		
			$	%	$		
			$	%	$		
			$	%	$		
			$	%	$		
			$	%	$		
			$	%	$		
			$	%	$		
			$	%	$		
		TOTALS	$		$		

Date	Category	Description	Other Parent's Payment	% Reimburse	I Owe	Date I Reimbursed	Notes
			$	%	$		
			$	%	$		
			$	%	$		
			$	%	$		
			$	%	$		
			$	%	$		
			$	%	$		
			$	%	$		
			$	%	$		
			$	%	$		
		TOTALS	$		$		

Date:_____

Date	Category	Description	My Payment Amount	% Reimburse	Other Parent Owes	Date Reimbursed	Notes
			$	%	$		
			$	%	$		
			$	%	$		
			$	%	$		
			$	%	$		
			$	%	$		
			$	%	$		
			$	%	$		
			$	%	$		
			$	%	$		
			$	%	$		
			$	%	$		
			$	%	$		
			$	%	$		
			$	%	$		
			$	%	$		
			$	%	$		
			$	%	$		
			$	%	$		
			$	%	$		
		TOTALS	$		$		

Date	Category	Description	Other Parent's Payment	% Reimburse	I Owe	Date I Reimbursed	Notes
			$	%	$		
			$	%	$		
			$	%	$		
			$	%	$		
			$	%	$		
			$	%	$		
			$	%	$		
			$	%	$		
			$	%	$		
			$	%	$		
		TOTALS	$		$		

Date:＿＿＿＿＿

Date	Category	Description	My Payment Amount	% Reimburse	Other Parent Owes	Date Reimbursed	Notes
			$	%	$		
			$	%	$		
			$	%	$		
			$	%	$		
			$	%	$		
			$	%	$		
			$	%	$		
			$	%	$		
			$	%	$		
			$	%	$		
			$	%	$		
			$	%	$		
			$	%	$		
			$	%	$		
			$	%	$		
			$	%	$		
			$	%	$		
			$	%	$		
			$	%	$		
			$	%	$		
		TOTALS	$		$		

Date	Category	Description	Other Parent's Payment	% Reimburse	I Owe	Date I Reimbursed	Notes
			$	%	$		
			$	%	$		
			$	%	$		
			$	%	$		
			$	%	$		
			$	%	$		
			$	%	$		
			$	%	$		
			$	%	$		
			$	%	$		
		TOTALS	$		$		

Date:_____

 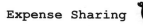

Date	Category	Description	My Payment Amount	% Reimburse	Other Parent Owes	Date Reimbursed	Notes
			$	%	$		
			$	%	$		
			$	%	$		
			$	%	$		
			$	%	$		
			$	%	$		
			$	%	$		
			$	%	$		
			$	%	$		
			$	%	$		
			$	%	$		
			$	%	$		
			$	%	$		
			$	%	$		
			$	%	$		
			$	%	$		
			$	%	$		
			$	%	$		
			$	%	$		
			$	%	$		
			$	%	$		
		TOTALS	$		$		

Date	Category	Description	Other Parent's Payment	% Reimburse	I Owe	Date I Reimbursed	Notes
			$	%	$		
			$	%	$		
			$	%	$		
			$	%	$		
			$	%	$		
			$	%	$		
			$	%	$		
			$	%	$		
			$	%	$		
			$	%	$		
		TOTALS	$		$		

Date:_____

Date	Category	Description	My Payment Amount	% Reimburse	Other Parent Owes	Date Reimbursed	Notes
			$	%	$		
			$	%	$		
			$	%	$		
			$	%	$		
			$	%	$		
			$	%	$		
			$	%	$		
			$	%	$		
			$	%	$		
			$	%	$		
			$	%	$		
			$	%	$		
			$	%	$		
			$	%	$		
			$	%	$		
			$	%	$		
			$	%	$		
			$	%	$		
			$	%	$		
			$	%	$		
TOTALS			$		$		

Date	Category	Description	Other Parent's Payment	% Reimburse	I Owe	Date I Reimbursed	Notes
			$	%	$		
			$	%	$		
			$	%	$		
			$	%	$		
			$	%	$		
			$	%	$		
			$	%	$		
			$	%	$		
			$	%	$		
			$	%	$		
TOTALS			$		$		

Date:_____

Date	Category	Description	My Payment Amount	% Reimburse	Other Parent Owes	Date Reimbursed	Notes
			$	%	$		
			$	%	$		
			$	%	$		
			$	%	$		
			$	%	$		
			$	%	$		
			$	%	$		
			$	%	$		
			$	%	$		
			$	%	$		
			$	%	$		
			$	%	$		
			$	%	$		
			$	%	$		
			$	%	$		
			$	%	$		
			$	%	$		
			$	%	$		
			$	%	$		
			$	%	$		
		TOTALS	$		$		

Date	Category	Description	Other Parent's Payment	% Reimburse	I Owe	Date I Reimbursed	Notes
			$	%	$		
			$	%	$		
			$	%	$		
			$	%	$		
			$	%	$		
			$	%	$		
			$	%	$		
			$	%	$		
			$	%	$		
		TOTALS	$		$		

Date:＿＿＿＿＿

Date	Category	Description	My Payment Amount	% Reimburse	Other Parent Owes	Date Reimbursed	Notes
			$	%	$		
			$	%	$		
			$	%	$		
			$	%	$		
			$	%	$		
			$	%	$		
			$	%	$		
			$	%	$		
			$	%	$		
			$	%	$		
			$	%	$		
			$	%	$		
			$	%	$		
			$	%	$		
			$	%	$		
			$	%	$		
			$	%	$		
			$	%	$		
			$	%	$		
			$	%	$		
		TOTALS	$		$		

Date	Category	Description	Other Parent's Payment	% Reimburse	I Owe	Date I Reimbursed	Notes
			$	%	$		
			$	%	$		
			$	%	$		
			$	%	$		
			$	%	$		
			$	%	$		
			$	%	$		
			$	%	$		
			$	%	$		
			$	%	$		
		TOTALS	$		$		

Date:_____

Date	Category	Description	My Payment Amount	% Reimburse	Other Parent Owes	Date Reimbursed	Notes
			$	%	$		
			$	%	$		
			$	%	$		
			$	%	$		
			$	%	$		
			$	%	$		
			$	%	$		
			$	%	$		
			$	%	$		
			$	%	$		
			$	%	$		
			$	%	$		
			$	%	$		
			$	%	$		
			$	%	$		
			$	%	$		
			$	%	$		
			$	%	$		
			$	%	$		
			$	%	$		
			$	%	$		
			$	%	$		
TOTALS			$		$		

Date	Category	Description	Other Parent's Payment	% Reimburse	I Owe	Date I Reimbursed	Notes
			$	%	$		
			$	%	$		
			$	%	$		
			$	%	$		
			$	%	$		
			$	%	$		
			$	%	$		
			$	%	$		
			$	%	$		
			$	%	$		
TOTALS			$		$		

Date:_____

 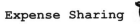

Date	Category	Description	My Payment Amount	% Reimburse	Other Parent Owes	Date Reimbursed	Notes
			$	%	$		
			$	%	$		
			$	%	$		
			$	%	$		
			$	%	$		
			$	%	$		
			$	%	$		
			$	%	$		
			$	%	$		
			$	%	$		
			$	%	$		
			$	%	$		
			$	%	$		
			$	%	$		
			$	%	$		
			$	%	$		
			$	%	$		
			$	%	$		
			$	%	$		
			$	%	$		
		TOTALS	$		$		

Date	Category	Description	Other Parent's Payment	% Reimburse	I Owe	Date I Reimbursed	Notes
			$	%	$		
			$	%	$		
			$	%	$		
			$	%	$		
			$	%	$		
			$	%	$		
			$	%	$		
			$	%	$		
			$	%	$		
			$	%	$		
		TOTALS	$		$		

Date:_____

Date	Category	Description	My Payment Amount	% Reimburse	Other Parent Owes	Date Reimbursed	Notes
			$	%	$		
			$	%	$		
			$	%	$		
			$	%	$		
			$	%	$		
			$	%	$		
			$	%	$		
			$	%	$		
			$	%	$		
			$	%	$		
			$	%	$		
			$	%	$		
			$	%	$		
			$	%	$		
			$	%	$		
			$	%	$		
			$	%	$		
			$	%	$		
			$	%	$		
			$	%	$		
			$	%	$		
TOTALS			$		$		

Date	Category	Description	Other Parent's Payment	% Reimburse	I Owe	Date I Reimbursed	Notes
			$	%	$		
			$	%	$		
			$	%	$		
			$	%	$		
			$	%	$		
			$	%	$		
			$	%	$		
			$	%	$		
			$	%	$		
			$	%	$		
TOTALS			$		$		

Date:_____

Date	Category	Description	My Payment Amount	% Reimburse	Other Parent Owes	Date Reimbursed	Notes
			$	%	$		
			$	%	$		
			$	%	$		
			$	%	$		
			$	%	$		
			$	%	$		
			$	%	$		
			$	%	$		
			$	%	$		
			$	%	$		
			$	%	$		
			$	%	$		
			$	%	$		
			$	%	$		
			$	%	$		
			$	%	$		
			$	%	$		
			$	%	$		
			$	%	$		
			$	%	$		
		TOTALS	$		$		

Date	Category	Description	Other Parent's Payment	% Reimburse	I Owe	Date I Reimbursed	Notes
			$	%	$		
			$	%	$		
			$	%	$		
			$	%	$		
			$	%	$		
			$	%	$		
			$	%	$		
			$	%	$		
			$	%	$		
			$	%	$		
		TOTALS	$		$		

Date:_____

Date	Category	Description	My Payment Amount	% Reimburse	Other Parent Owes	Date Reimbursed	Notes
			$	%	$		
			$	%	$		
			$	%	$		
			$	%	$		
			$	%	$		
			$	%	$		
			$	%	$		
			$	%	$		
			$	%	$		
			$	%	$		
			$	%	$		
			$	%	$		
			$	%	$		
			$	%	$		
			$	%	$		
			$	%	$		
			$	%	$		
			$	%	$		
			$	%	$		
			$	%	$		
			$	%	$		
TOTALS			$		$		

Date	Category	Description	Other Parent's Payment	% Reimburse	I Owe	Date I Reimbursed	Notes
			$	%	$		
			$	%	$		
			$	%	$		
			$	%	$		
			$	%	$		
			$	%	$		
			$	%	$		
			$	%	$		
			$	%	$		
			$	%	$		
TOTALS			$		$		

Date:_____

Date	Category	Description	My Payment Amount	% Reimburse	Other Parent Owes	Date Reimbursed	Notes
			$	%	$		
			$	%	$		
			$	%	$		
			$	%	$		
			$	%	$		
			$	%	$		
			$	%	$		
			$	%	$		
			$	%	$		
			$	%	$		
			$	%	$		
			$	%	$		
			$	%	$		
			$	%	$		
			$	%	$		
			$	%	$		
			$	%	$		
			$	%	$		
			$	%	$		
			$	%	$		
			$	%	$		
		TOTALS	$		$		

Date	Category	Description	Other Parent's Payment	% Reimburse	I Owe	Date I Reimbursed	Notes
			$	%	$		
			$	%	$		
			$	%	$		
			$	%	$		
			$	%	$		
			$	%	$		
			$	%	$		
			$	%	$		
			$	%	$		
			$	%	$		
		TOTALS	$		$		

Date:_____

 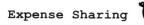

Date	Category	Description	My Payment Amount	% Reimburse	Other Parent Owes	Date Reimbursed	Notes
			$	%	$		
			$	%	$		
			$	%	$		
			$	%	$		
			$	%	$		
			$	%	$		
			$	%	$		
			$	%	$		
			$	%	$		
			$	%	$		
			$	%	$		
			$	%	$		
			$	%	$		
			$	%	$		
			$	%	$		
			$	%	$		
			$	%	$		
			$	%	$		
			$	%	$		
			$	%	$		
		TOTALS	$		$		

Date	Category	Description	Other Parent's Payment	% Reimburse	I Owe	Date I Reimbursed	Notes
			$	%	$		
			$	%	$		
			$	%	$		
			$	%	$		
			$	%	$		
			$	%	$		
			$	%	$		
			$	%	$		
			$	%	$		
			$	%	$		
		TOTALS	$		$		

Date:_____

 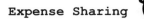

Date	Category	Description	My Payment Amount	% Reimburse	Other Parent Owes	Date Reimbursed	Notes
			$	%	$		
			$	%	$		
			$	%	$		
			$	%	$		
			$	%	$		
			$	%	$		
			$	%	$		
			$	%	$		
			$	%	$		
			$	%	$		
			$	%	$		
			$	%	$		
			$	%	$		
			$	%	$		
			$	%	$		
			$	%	$		
			$	%	$		
			$	%	$		
			$	%	$		
			$	%	$		
		TOTALS	$		$		

Date	Category	Description	Other Parent's Payment	% Reimburse	I Owe	Date I Reimbursed	Notes
			$	%	$		
			$	%	$		
			$	%	$		
			$	%	$		
			$	%	$		
			$	%	$		
			$	%	$		
			$	%	$		
			$	%	$		
			$	%	$		
		TOTALS	$		$		

Communication Logs

Date:_____

 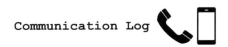

Date	Time	a.m./p.m.	Notes

Date:_____

 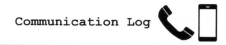

Date	Time	a.m./p.m.	Notes

Date:_____

 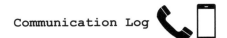

Date	Time	a.m./p.m.	Notes

Date:_____

 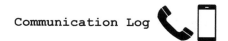

Date	Time	a.m./p.m.	Notes

Date:_____

 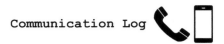

Date	Time	a.m./p.m.	Notes

Date:_____

 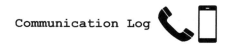

Date	Time	a.m./p.m.	Notes

Date:_____

 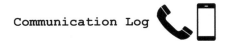

Date	Time	a.m./p.m.	Notes

Date:_____

Date	Time	a.m./p.m.	Notes

Date:_____

 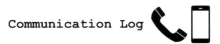

Date	Time	a.m./p.m.	Notes

Date:_____

 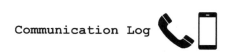

Date	Time	a.m./p.m.	Notes

Date:_____

 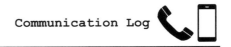

Date	Time	a.m./p.m.	Notes

Date:_____

Date	Time	a.m./p.m.	Notes

Date:_____

 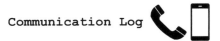

Date	Time	a.m./p.m.	Notes

Date:_____

 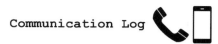

Date	Time	a.m./p.m.	Notes

Date:_____

 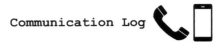

Date	Time	a.m./p.m.	Notes

Date:＿＿＿＿＿

Communication Log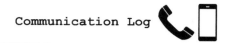

Date	Time	a.m./p.m.	Notes

Date:_____

Date	Time	a.m./p.m.	Notes

Event Trackers

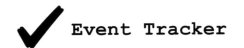 **Event Tracker**

Date : _____
Event:_____

Month / Day														
1														
2														
3														
4														
5														
6														
7														
8														
9														
10														
11														
12														
13														
14														
15														
16														
17														
18														
19														
20														
21														
22														
23														
24														
25														
26														
27														
28														
29														
30														
31														

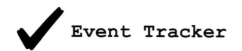 **Event Tracker**

Date :_____

Event:_____

Month / Day															
1															
2															
3															
4															
5															
6															
7															
8															
9															
10															
11															
12															
13															
14															
15															
16															
17															
18															
19															
20															
21															
22															
23															
24															
25															
26															
27															
28															
29															
30															
31															

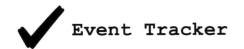 **Event Tracker**

Date : _____

Event: _____

Month Day	/	/	/	/	/	/	/	/	/	/	/	/	/	/
1														
2														
3														
4														
5														
6														
7														
8														
9														
10														
11														
12														
13														
14														
15														
16														
17														
18														
19														
20														
21														
22														
23														
24														
25														
26														
27														
28														
29														
30														
31														

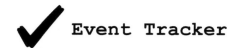 **Event Tracker**

Date : _____

Event: _____

Month Day															
1															
2															
3															
4															
5															
6															
7															
8															
9															
10															
11															
12															
13															
14															
15															
16															
17															
18															
19															
20															
21															
22															
23															
24															
25															
26															
27															
28															
29															
30															
31															

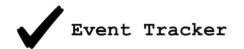 **Event Tracker**

Date : _____

Event: _____

Month Day															
1															
2															
3															
4															
5															
6															
7															
8															
9															
10															
11															
12															
13															
14															
15															
16															
17															
18															
19															
20															
21															
22															
23															
24															
25															
26															
27															
28															
29															
30															
31															

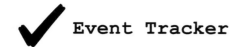 **Event Tracker**

Date : _____

Event: _____

Month / Day															
1															
2															
3															
4															
5															
6															
7															
8															
9															
10															
11															
12															
13															
14															
15															
16															
17															
18															
19															
20															
21															
22															
23															
24															
25															
26															
27															
28															
29															
30															
31															

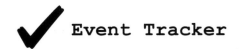 **Event Tracker**

Date : _____
Event: _____

Month Day																
1																
2																
3																
4																
5																
6																
7																
8																
9																
10																
11																
12																
13																
14																
15																
16																
17																
18																
19																
20																
21																
22																
23																
24																
25																
26																
27																
28																
29																
30																
31																

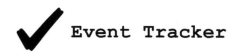 **Event Tracker**

Date :_____

Event:_____

Month Day															
1															
2															
3															
4															
5															
6															
7															
8															
9															
10															
11															
12															
13															
14															
15															
16															
17															
18															
19															
20															
21															
22															
23															
24															
25															
26															
27															
28															
29															
30															
31															

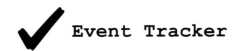 **Event Tracker**

Date : _____

Event: _____

Month Day															
1															
2															
3															
4															
5															
6															
7															
8															
9															
10															
11															
12															
13															
14															
15															
16															
17															
18															
19															
20															
21															
22															
23															
24															
25															
26															
27															
28															
29															
30															
31															

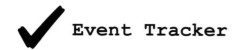 **Event Tracker**

Date :_____

Event:_____

Month Day																
1																
2																
3																
4																
5																
6																
7																
8																
9																
10																
11																
12																
13																
14																
15																
16																
17																
18																
19																
20																
21																
22																
23																
24																
25																
26																
27																
28																
29																
30																
31																

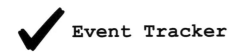 **Event Tracker**

Date : _____

Event: _____

Month Day															
1															
2															
3															
4															
5															
6															
7															
8															
9															
10															
11															
12															
13															
14															
15															
16															
17															
18															
19															
20															
21															
22															
23															
24															
25															
26															
27															
28															
29															
30															
31															

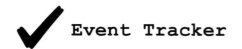 **Event Tracker**

Date :_____

Event:_____

Month / Day																
1																
2																
3																
4																
5																
6																
7																
8																
9																
10																
11																
12																
13																
14																
15																
16																
17																
18																
19																
20																
21																
22																
23																
24																
25																
26																
27																
28																
29																
30																
31																

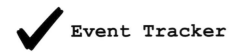 **Event Tracker**

Date :_____

Event:_____

Month / Day														
1														
2														
3														
4														
5														
6														
7														
8														
9														
10														
11														
12														
13														
14														
15														
16														
17														
18														
19														
20														
21														
22														
23														
24														
25														
26														
27														
28														
29														
30														
31														

Dependents

Dependents by Tax Year

Tax Year	Child	Parent	Notes

Dependents by Tax Year

Tax Year	Child	Parent	Notes

Dependents by Tax Year

Tax Year	Child	Parent	Notes

January Daily

January 1

January 2

January 3

January 4

January 5

January 6

January 7

January 8

January 9

January 10

January 11

January 12

January 13

January 14

January 15

January 16

January 17

January 18

January 19

January 20

January 21

January 22

January 23

January 24

January 25

January 26

January 27

January 28

January 29

January 30

January 31

Notes

February Daily

February 1

February 2

February 3

February 4

February 5

February 6

February 7

February 8

February 9

February 10

February 11

February 12

February 13

February 14

February 15

February 16

February 17

February 18

February 19

February 20

February 21

February 22

February 23

February 24

February 25

February 26

February 27

February 28

February 29

Notes

Notes

March Daily

March 1

March 2

March 3

March 4

March 5

March 6

March 7

March 8

March 9

March 10

March 11

March 12

March 13

March 14

March 15

March 16

March 17

March 18

March 19

March 20

March 21

March 22

March 23

March 24

March 25

March 26

March 27

March 28

March 29

March 30

March 31

Notes

April Daily

April 1

April 2

April 3

April 4

April 5

April 6

April 7

April 8

April 9

April 10

April 11

April 12

April 13

April 14

April 15

April 16

April 17

April 18

April 19

April 20

April 21

April 22

April 23

April 24

April 25

April 26

April 27

April 28

April 29

April 30

Notes

Notes

May Daily

May 1

May 2

May 3

May 4

May 5

May 6

May 7

May 8

May 9

May 10

May 11

May 12

May 13

May 14

May 15

May 16

May 17

May 18

May 19

May 20

May 21

May 22

May 23

May 24

May 25

May 26

May 27

May 28

May 29

May 30

May 31

Notes

June Daily

June 1

June 2

June 3

June 4

June 5

June 6

June 7

June 8

June 9

June 10

June 11

June 12

June 13

June 14

June 15

June 16

June 17

June 18

June 19

June 20

June 21

June 22

June 23

June 24

June 25

June 26

June 27

June 28

June 29

June 30

Notes

Notes

July Daily

July 1

July 2

July 3

July 4

July 5

July 6

July 7

July 8

July 9

July 10

July 11

July 12

July 13

July 14

July 15

July 16

July 17

July 18

July 19

July 20

July 21

July 22

July 23

July 24

July 25

July 26

July 27

July 28

July 29

July 30

July 31

Notes

August Daily

August 1

August 2

August 3

August 4

August 5

August 6

August 7

August 8

August 9

August 10

August 11

August 12

August 13

August 14

August 15

August 16

August 17

August 18

August 19

August 20

August 21

August 22

August 23

August 24

August 25

August 26

August 27

August 28

August 29

August 30

August 31

Notes

September Daily

September 1

September 2

September 3

September 4

September 5

September 6

September 7

September 8

September 9

September 10

September 11

September 12

September 13

September 14

September 15

September 16

September 17

September 18

September 19

September 20

September 21

September 22

September 23

September 24

September 25

September 26

September 27

September 28

September 29

September 30

Notes

Notes

October Daily

October 1

October 2

October 3

October 4

October 5

October 6

October 7

October 8

October 9

October 10

October 11

October 12

October 13

October 14

October 15

October 16

October 17

October 18

October 19

October 20

October 21

October 22

October 23

October 24

October 25

October 26

October 27

October 28

October 29

October 30

October 31

Notes

November Daily

November 1

November 2

November 3

November 4

November 5

November 6

November 7

November 8

November 9

November 10

November 11

November 12

November 13

November 14

November 15

November 16

November 17

November 18

November 19

November 20

November 21

November 22

November 23

November 24

November 25

November 26

November 27

November 28

November 29

November 30

Notes

Notes

December Daily

December 1

December 2

December 3

December 4

December 5

December 6

December 7

December 8

December 9

December 10

December 11

December 12

December 13

December 14

December 15

December 16

December 17

December 18

December 19

December 20

December 21

December 22

December 23

December 24

December 25

December 26

December 27

December 28

December 29

December 30

December 31

Notes

Notes

Notes

Notes

Notes

Notes

Notes

Made in United States
Orlando, FL
19 March 2023

31204899R00198